W9-AZH-919

SUMMER LINK

MATH *plus* READING

American Education Publishing™
An imprint of Carson-Dellosa Publishing LLC
Greensboro, North Carolina

American Education Publishing™
An imprint of Carson-Dellosa Publishing LLC
P.O. Box 35665
Greensboro, NC 27425 USA

Table of Contents
by Section

Summer Link Math
Table of Contents

Summer Link Reading
Table of Contents

This page intentionally left blank.

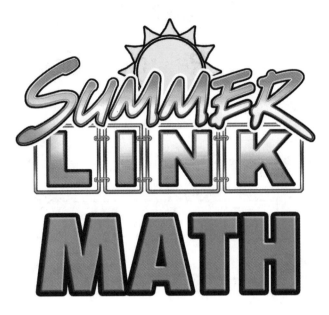

MATH

Name _____

Number Recognition

Directions: Write the numbers 1–10. Color the bear.

Name _____

Zero

Directions: Color the tank to show that it has 0 fish. Color the tanks that have 0 fish.

 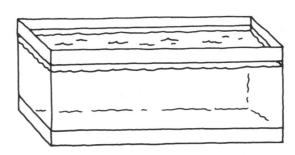

 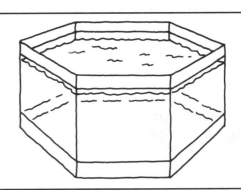

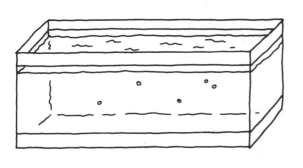 

Summer Link Super Edition Grade 1

Name _____

One and Two

Directions: Count how many cars are on each track. Circle the number that shows how many.

Three

Directions: Color the 3 kittens in the basket. Color 3 animals in each group.

3

Summer Link Super Edition Grade 1

Name _____

Four

Directions: Color the 4 crayons. Count how many. Circle the correct number.

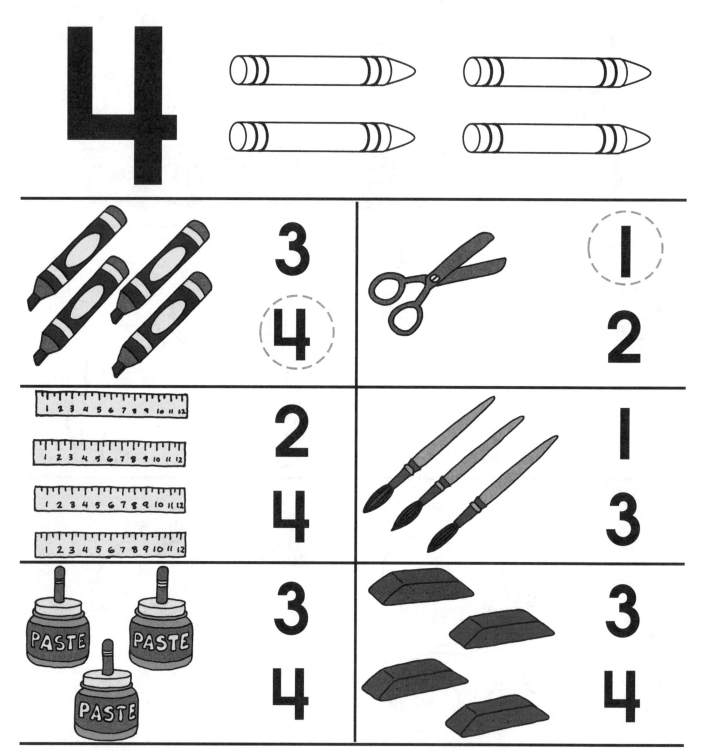

Five

Directions: Color the 5 party hats. Color and circle the groups that have 5.

5

Review Numbers 1-5

Directions: Look at the picture. Read the questions. Circle the correct number.

◆ How many in all? 3 4 5

◆ How many in all? 3 4 5

◆ How many in all? 3 4 5

Review Numbers 1-5

Directions: Draw a line from the number to the group that matches it.

1

2

3

4

5

Six

Directions: Look at the number 6. Count the teddy bears. Trace the circle to show this is a group of 6. Circle the group if it shows 6.

Name _____

Review Numbers 1-6

Directions: Count each group of blocks. Trace each number. Count each group of blocks below. Write the number.

Seven

Directions: Look at the number 7. Count how many bees. Color the 7 bees. Count how many. Circle the number.

7

6

(7)

(4)

5

5

7

6

7

6

7

5

7

Eight

Directions: Look at the number 8. Count the envelopes. Trace the circle to show this is a group of 8. Circle the group if it shows 8.

  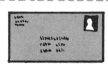 

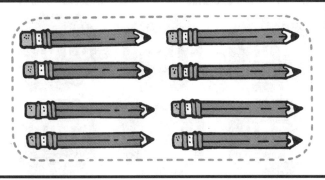

Nine

Directions: Look at the number 9. Circle 9 cars. Circle the signs to show the number.

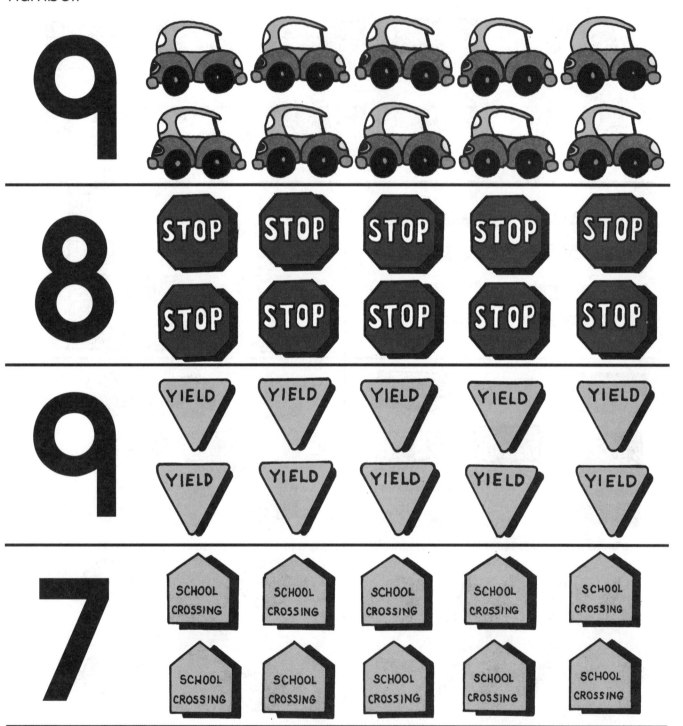

Ten

Directions: Look at the number 10. Trace the circle to show this is a group of 10. Circle each group of 10 objects.

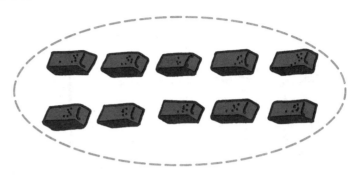

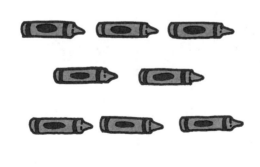

Nine and Ten

Directions: Count and write the number in each box. Circle the groups of 9. Color the groups of 10.

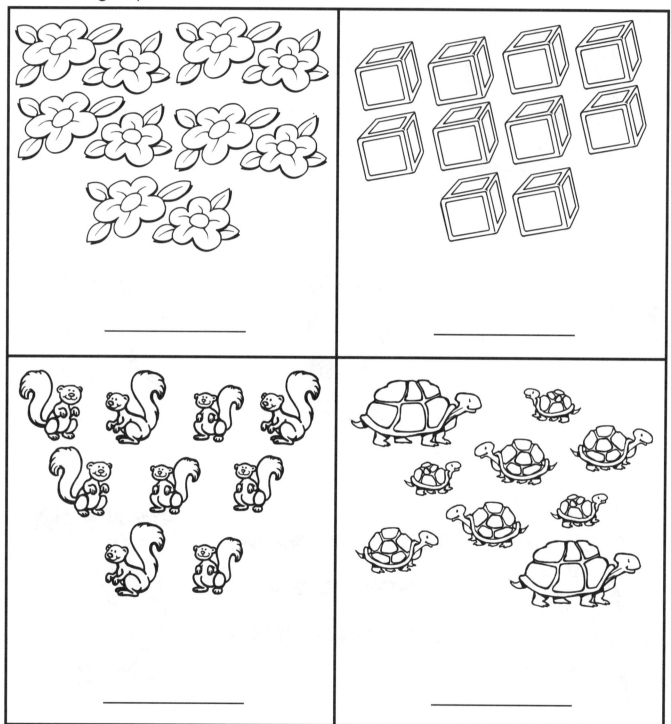

Review Numbers 7-10

Directions: Count each group of balloons. Trace each number. Count each group of balloons below. Write the number.

Eleven and Twelve

Directions: Trace and write the numbers 11 and 12. Count and write the numbers.

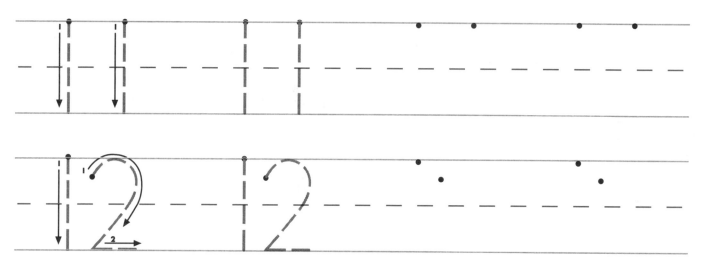

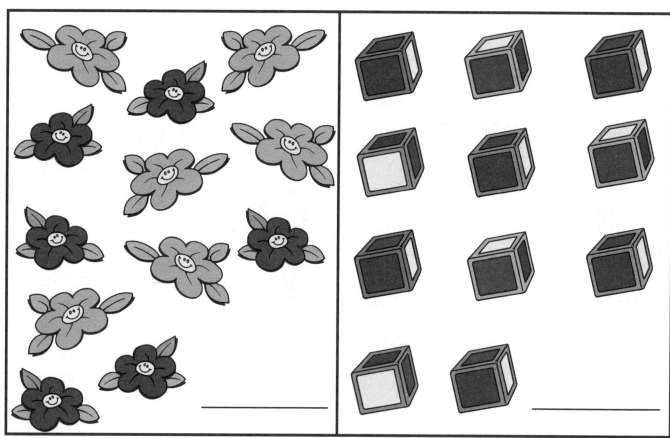

Name _____

Eleven and Twelve

Directions: Draw flowers to show the number in each box.

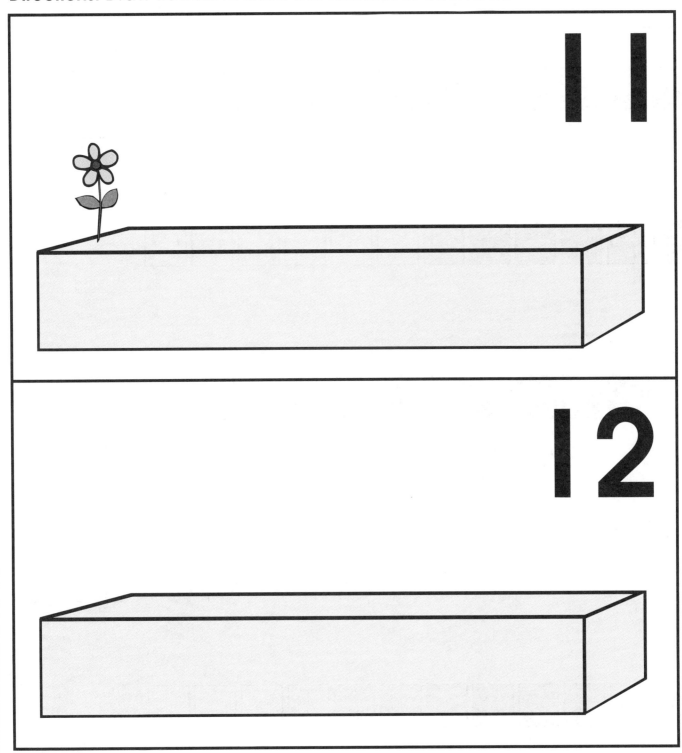

Review Numbers 1-12

Directions: Count the number of colored squares. Then write the correct number.

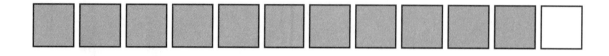

_____

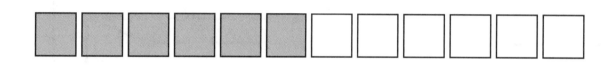

_____

_____

_____

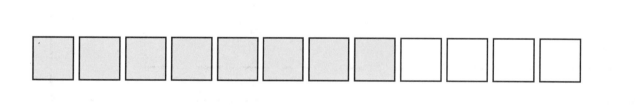

_____

Name _____

Thirteen

Directions: Trace and write the number 13. Complete each puzzle by writing or drawing the missing number of flowers.

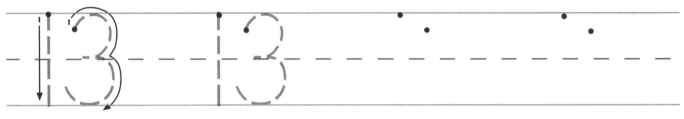

27   **Summer Link Super Edition Grade 1**

Fourteen

Directions: Trace and write the number 14.
Connect the dots. Color the picture. What is it?

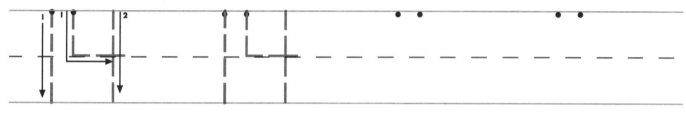

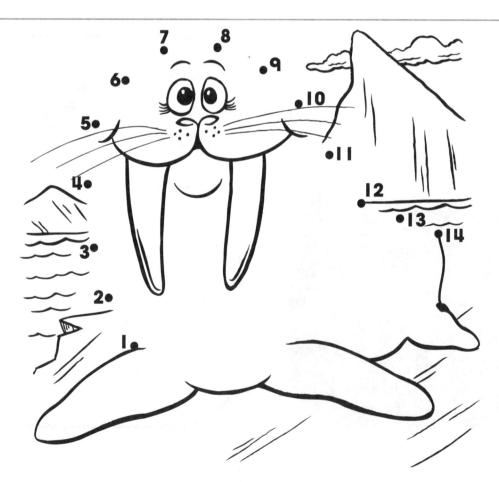

Summer Link Super Edition Grade 1

28

Fifteen

Directions: Trace and write the number 15. Write the missing pool ball numbers.

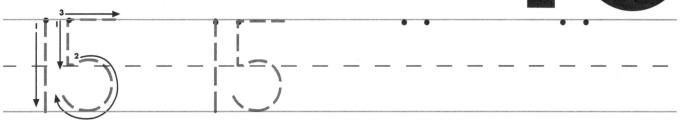

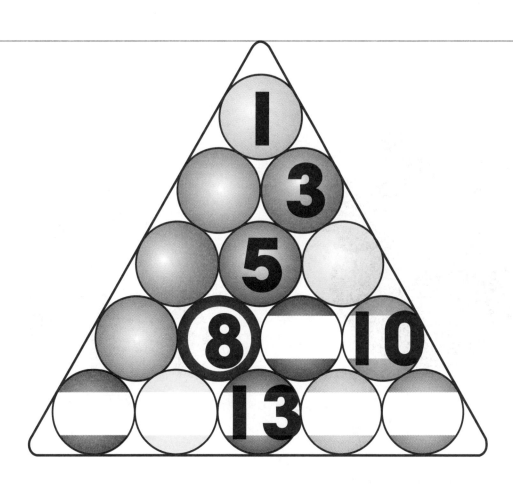

Sixteen

Directions: Trace and write the number 16. Draw eight legs on each spider.

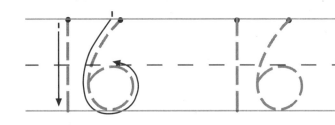

How many legs are there in all? _____

Seventeen

Directions: Trace and write the number 17. Circle each group of 17 things. Color the dog.

Name _____

Eighteen

Directions: Trace and write the number 18. Help Filbert Fish find his way to the top. Write the numbers 1–18 in each bubble along the way.

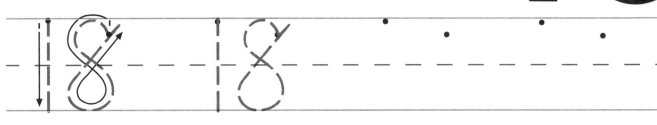

Name _____

Nineteen

Directions: Trace and write the number 19. Circle the numbers 1–19 in the picture.

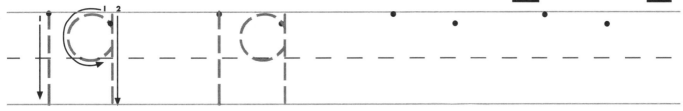

Twenty

Directions: Trace and write the number 20.
Connect the dots to find the hidden picture.
What is it?

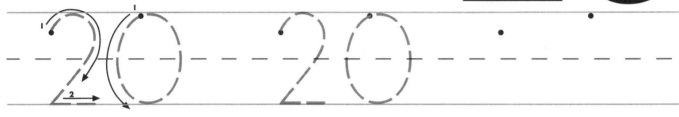

5• •8

14•

15•

9• 10

•11

4•

•12 •13

•16

•17

•18

3•

•19

2•

20

1•

Number Recognition

Directions: Count the number of objects in each group. Draw a line to the correct number.

1

2

3

4

5

6

7

8

9

10

Number Words

Directions: Number the buildings from one to six.

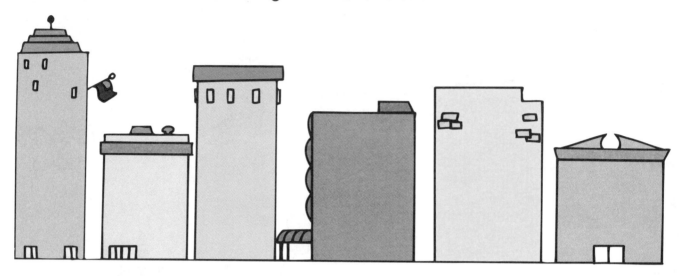

Directions: Draw a line from the word to the number.

two	1
five	3
six	5
four	6
one	2
three	4

Number Words

Directions: Number the buildings from five to ten.

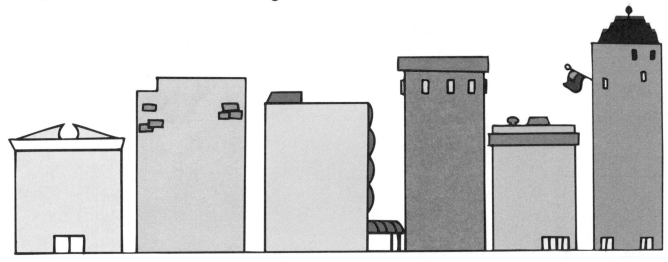

Directions: Draw a line from the word to the number.

nine	**8**
seven	**10**
five	**7**
eight	**5**
six	**9**
ten	**6**

Sequencing Numbers

Sequencing is putting numbers in the correct order.

1, 2, 3, 4, 5, 6, 7, 8, 9, 10

Directions: Write the missing numbers.

Example: 4, ___5___ , 6

3, _____ ,5   7, _____ ,9   8, _____ ,10

6, _____ ,8   _____ ,3, 4   _____ ,5, 6

5, 6, _____   _____ ,6, 7   _____ ,3, 4

_____ ,4, 5   _____ ,7, 8   5, _____ ,7

2, 3, _____   1, 2, _____   7, 8, _____

2, _____ ,4   _____ ,2, 3   4, _____ ,6

6, 7, _____   3, 4, _____   1, _____ ,3

7, 8, _____   _____ ,3, 4   _____ ,9, 10

Name _____

Review

Directions: Count the objects and write the number.

- - - - - - - - -   - - - - - - - - -   - - - - - - - - -

Directions: Match the number to the word.

two	1
four	9
seven	2
three	3
one	4
nine	7

Name _____

Ordinal Numbers

Ordinal numbers are used to indicate order in a series, such as **first, second,** or **third.**

Directions: Draw a line to the picture that goes with the ordinal number in the left column.

eighth

third

sixth

ninth

seventh

second

fourth

first

fifth

tenth

1st

7th

10th

2nd

4th

6th

8th

9th

3rd

5th

Ordinal Numbers

Directions: Color the first leaf red. Circle the third leaf.

Directions: Color the fourth balloon purple. Draw a line under the second balloon.

Name _____

Orderly Ordinals

Directions: Write each word on the correct line to put the words in order.

second	fifth	seventh	first	tenth
third	eighth	sixth	fourth	ninth

1. _____   6. _____

2. _____   7. _____

3. _____   8. _____

4. _____   9. _____

5. _____   10. _____

Directions: Which picture is circled in each row? Underline the word that tells the correct number.

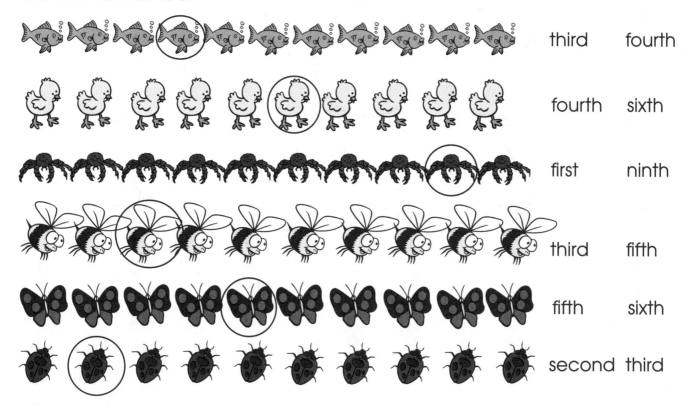

third   fourth

fourth   sixth

first   ninth

third   fifth

fifth   sixth

second   third

Name _____

One for Each

Directions: Each circus seal needs one ball. Draw a ball for each seal.

Summer Link Super Edition Grade 1

Name _____

More

Directions: Circle the group in each box that has more.

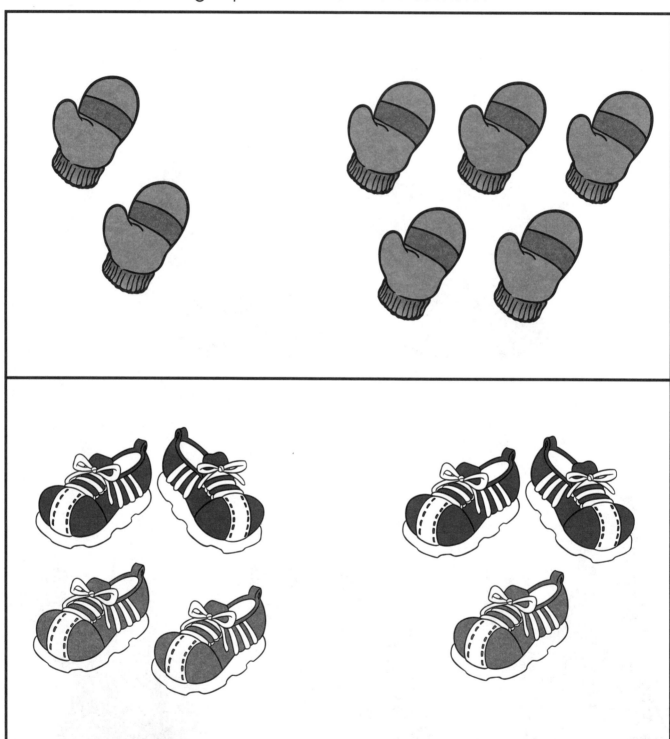

More

Directions: Trace the lines to match the rows of mittens one-to-one. Circle the 6 to show that 6 is more than 4. Match the objects one-to-one. Circle the number that is more.

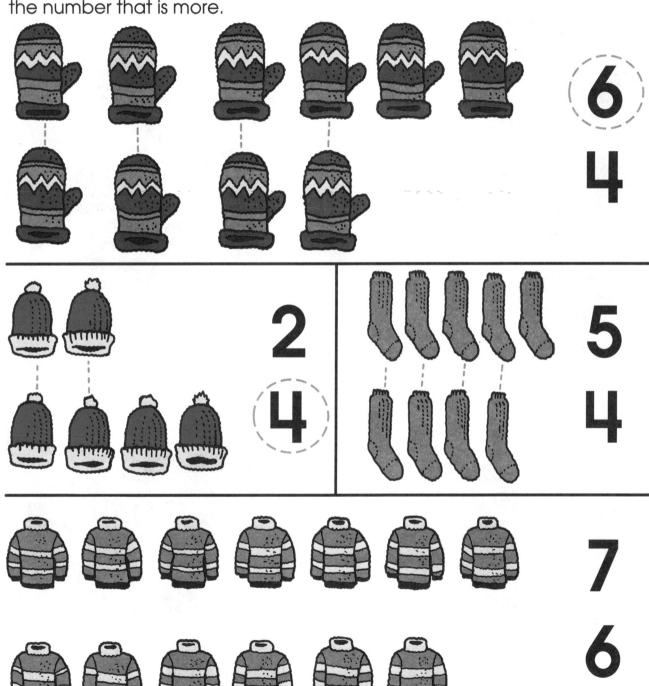

Name _____

Less

Directions: Circle the group in each box that has less.

Name _____

Less

Directions: Trace the lines to match the fish one-to-one. Circle the 4 to show that 4 is less than 6. Match the objects one-to-one. Circle the number that is less.

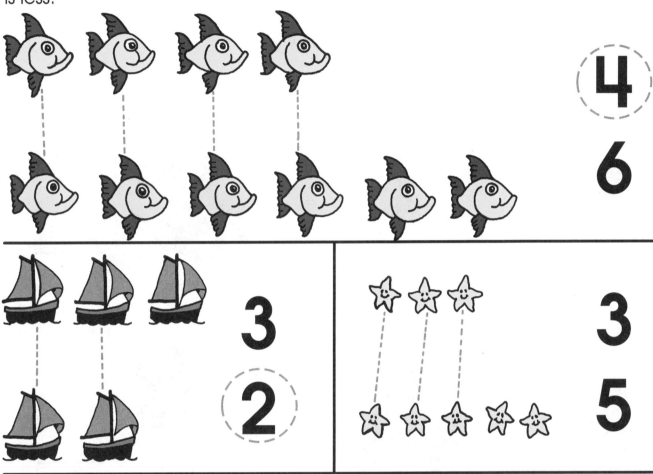

Summer Link Super Edition Grade 1

Addition 1, 2

Addition means "putting together" or adding two or more numbers to find the sum. "+" is a plus sign. It means to add the 2 numbers. "=" is an equals sign. It tells how much they are together.

Directions: Count the cats and tell how many.

 +  =  _____

 =  _____

 _____

Addition

Directions: Count the shapes and write the numbers below to tell how many in all.

 + =

- - - - - - -   - - - - - - -   - - - - - - -

 + 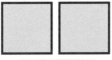 =

- - - - - - -   - - - - - - -   - - - - - - -

 =

- - - - - - -   - - - - - - -   - - - - - - -

 =

- - - - - - -   - - - - - - -   - - - - - - -

49   Summer Link Super Edition Grade 1

Picture Problems: Addition

Directions: Solve the number problem under each picture.

 +

6 + 2 = ____

3 + 1 = ____

 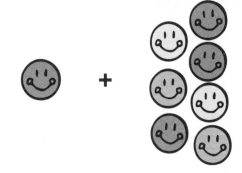

5 + 3 = ____

1 + 7 = ____

 +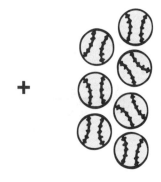

4 + 5 = ____

0 + 7 = ____

How Many in All?

Directions: Count the number in each group and write the number on the line. Then, add the groups together and write the sum.

 _____ strawberries

 _____ strawberries

How many in all? _____

 _____ cookies

 _____ cookies

How many in all? _____

 _____ shoes

 _____ shoes

How many in all? _____

 _____ balloons

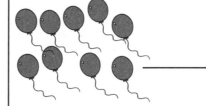 _____ balloons

How many in all? _____

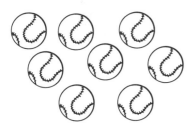 _____ balls

 _____ balls

How many in all? _____

 _____ flowers

 _____ flowers

How many in all? _____

Subtraction 1, 2, 3

Subtraction means "taking away" or subtracting one number from another. "−" is a minus sign. It means to subtract the second number from the first.

Directions: Practice writing the numbers and then subtract. Draw dots and cross them out, if needed.

1 -

2 -

3 -

$$3 - 1 = 2$$

$$4 - 3$$

$$2 - 1$$

$$3 - 2$$

Name _____

Picture Problems: Subtraction

Directions: Solve the number problem under each picture.

5 – 2 = _____

6 – 1 = _____

7 – 4 = _____

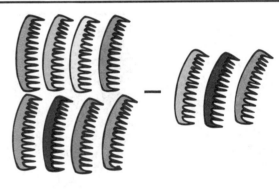

8 – 3 = _____

9 – 2 = _____

4 – 4 = _____

Summer Link Super Edition Grade 1

Name _____

Picture Problems: Addition and Subtraction

Directions: Solve the number problem under each picture.

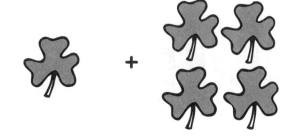

7 – 4 = ____   I + 4 = ____

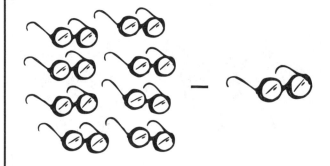

3 + 5 = ____   8 – I = ____

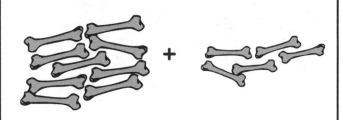

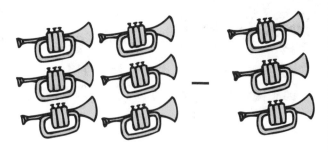

9 + 5 = ____   6 – 3 = ____

Name _____

Review: Addition and Subtraction

Directions: Solve the number problem under each picture. Write + or – to show if you should add or subtract.

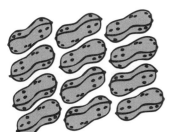

How many s are left?

12 ___ 4 = ____

How many 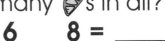s in all?

6 ___ 8 = ____

How many s are left?

4 ___ 4 = ____

How many s are left?

11 ___ 7 = ____

How many 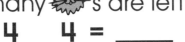s in all?

9 ___ 3 = ____

How many s in all?

10 ___ 0 = ____

Summer Link Super Edition Grade 1

Name _____

Addition and Subtraction

Directions: Solve the problems. Remember, addition means "putting together" or adding two or more numbers to find the sum. Subtraction means "taking away" or subtracting one number from another.

1 + 3 = ___   4 – 3 = ___   4 + 5 = ___

6 + 1 = ___   7 – 2 = ___   8 – 4 = ___

9 – 1 = ___   10 – 3 = ___

 5 – 2 = ___   6 + 3 = ___

8 + 2 = ___   5 + 5 = ___

Nickels

Directions: A nickel is worth 5¢. It is silver. Circle the correct amount of money in each row below.

Example:

 =

5¢   5¢

4¢   5¢   6¢

1¢   2¢   3¢

1¢   2¢   3¢

Name _____

Nickels

Directions: Circle the correct amount of money in each row below.

     3¢ 4¢ 5¢

 **4¢ 5¢ 6¢**

    3¢ 4¢ 5¢

   4¢ 5¢ 6¢

Summer Link Super Edition Grade 1   64

Dimes

Directions: A dime is worth 10¢. It is silver. Circle the correct amount of money in each row below.

Example:

 = =

10¢   10¢   10¢

          1¢   5¢   10¢

          5¢   7¢   10¢

          8¢   9¢   10¢

Name _____

Dimes

Directions: Circle the correct amount of money in each row below.

2¢ 3¢ 4¢

5¢ 6¢ 7¢

8¢ 9¢ 10¢

9¢ 10¢ 11¢

Review Money

Directions: Match the price of each thing to the correct amount of money.

 2¢

 10¢

 5¢

Review Money

Directions: Match the coins to the correct amount of money.

                                     10¢

                                     5¢

                                                          2¢

                                                         6¢

   **1¢**

                                                          8¢

Shapes: Square

A square is a figure with four corners and four sides of the same length.

This is a square 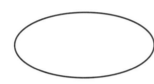 .

Directions: Find the squares and circle them.

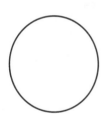

Directions: Trace the word. Write the word.

square

Name _____

Shapes: Circle

A circle is a figure that is round. This is a circle ○.

Directions: Find the circles and put a square around them.

Directions: Trace the word. Write the word.

circle

Shapes: Square and Circle

Directions: Practice drawing squares. Trace the samples and make four of your own.

Directions: Practice drawing circles. Trace the samples and make four of your own.

Name _____

Shapes: Triangle

A triangle is a figure with three corners and three sides.

This is a triangle △ .

Directions: Find the triangles and put a circle around them.

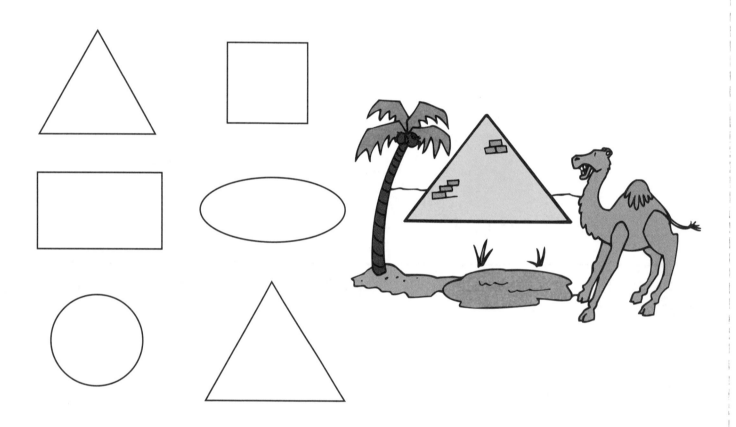

Directions: Trace the word. Write the word.

triangle -

Name _____

Shapes: Rectangle

A rectangle is a figure with four corners and four sides. Sides opposite each other are the same length.

This is a rectangle .

Directions: Find the rectangles and put a circle around them.

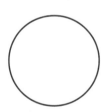
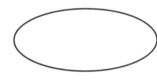

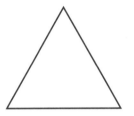

Directions: Trace the word. Write the word.

rectangle

Shapes: Triangle and Rectangle

Directions: Practice drawing triangles. Trace the samples and make four of your own.

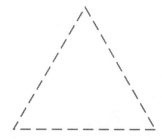

Directions: Practice drawing rectangles. Trace the samples and make four of your own.

Name _____

Shapes: Oval and Diamond

An oval is an egg-shaped figure. A diamond is a figure with four sides of the same length. Its corners form points at the top, sides, and bottom.

This is an oval ⬯.   This is a diamond ◇.

Directions: Color the ovals red. Color the diamonds blue.

Directions: Trace the words. Write the words.

oval

diamond

Summer Link Super Edition Grade 1

Shapes: Oval and Diamond

Directions: Practice drawing ovals. Trace the samples and make four of your own.

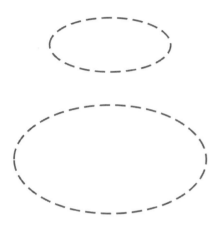

Directions: Practice drawing diamonds. Trace the samples and make four of your own.

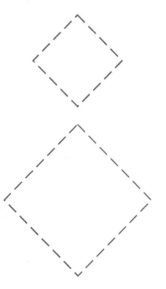

Animal Shapes

Directions: Color: squares — green   rectangles — yellow
circles — red   triangles — blue

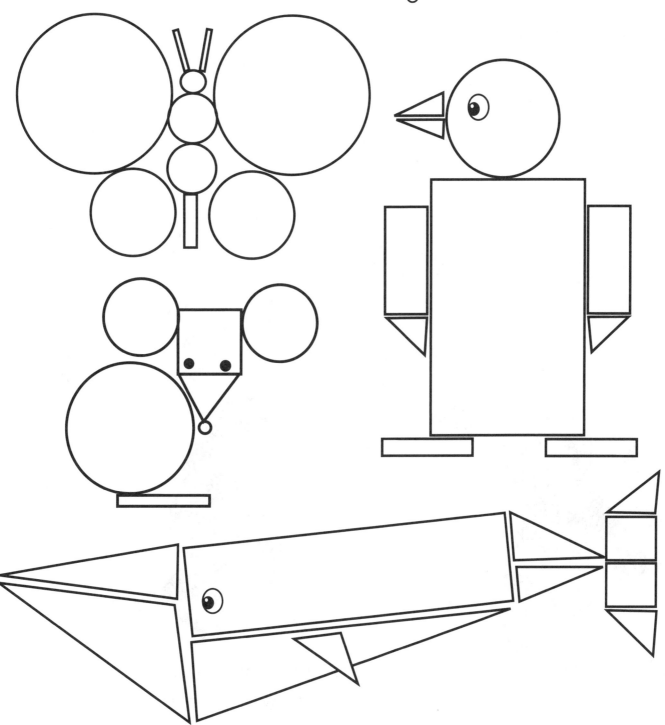

Name _____

Classifying: Shapes

Mary and Rudy are taking a trip into space. Help them find the stars, moons, circles, and diamonds.

Directions: Color the shapes.

Use yellow for ☆s.   Use blue for ☾s.

Use red for ○s.   Use purple for ◇s.

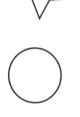
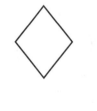

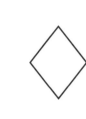

How many stars? _____   How many moons? _____

How many circles? _____   How many diamonds? _____

Summer Link Super Edition Grade 1   78

Same Shape

Directions: Look at the round shapes. They are all the same shape. Draw a line from each shape in the bottom row to the box with the same shape.

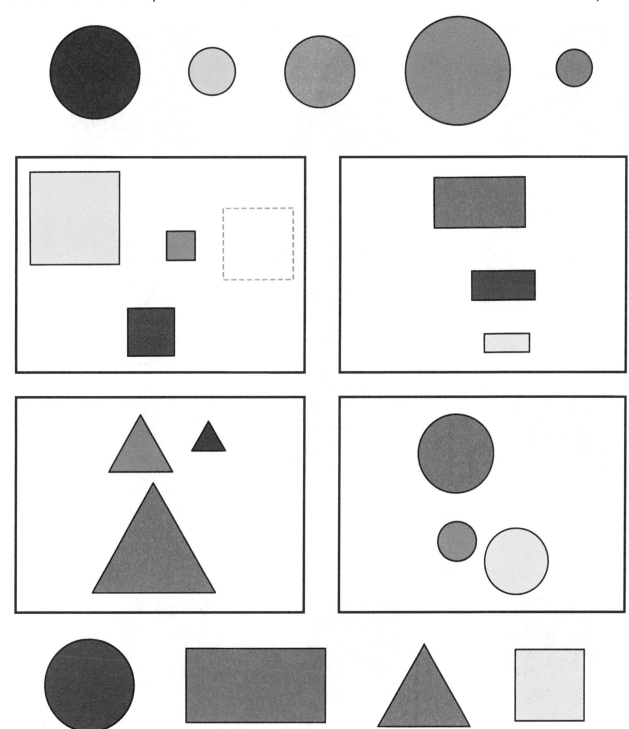

Name _____

Different

Directions: Circle the shape that is different. Circle the object in each row that is different.

 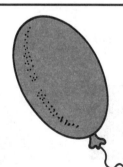 

Summer Link Super Edition Grade 1   80

Name _____

Patterns

Directions: Draw what comes next in each pattern.

Example:

   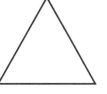 

 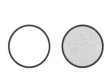

Summer Link Super Edition Grade 1

Name _____

Patterns

Directions: Fill in the missing shape in each row. Then color it.

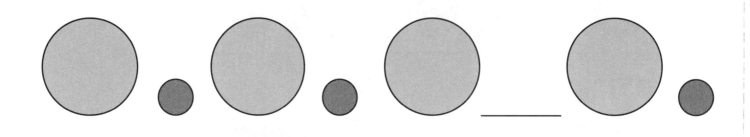

_____

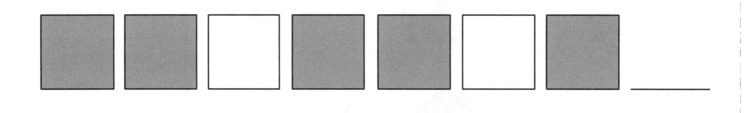

_____

_____

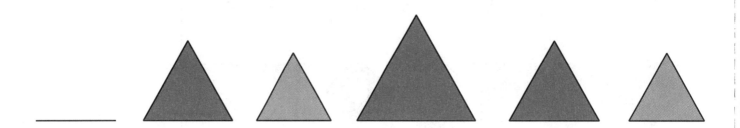

Graphing

Directions: How many fire engines did the children have? Count the boxes. Write the number. How many of each vehicle? Count the boxes. Write the numbers.

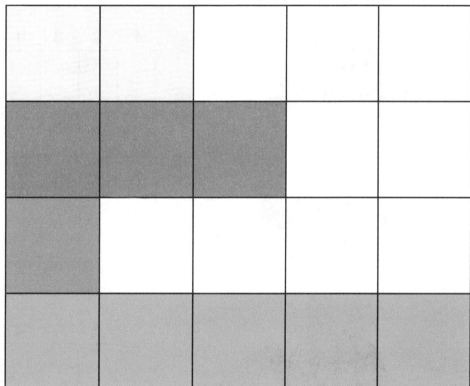

 2

Summer Link Super Edition Grade 1

Name _____

Graphing

Directions: Count the spots on the turtles. Color the boxes to show how many spots each turtle has.

1	2	3	4	5	6	7	8

1	2	3	4	5	6	7	8

1	2	3	4	5	6	7	8

1	2	3	4	5	6	7	8

1	2	3	4	5	6	7	8

Graphing

Directions: Count the shapes in the picture. Then complete the graph below.

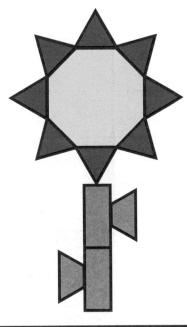

8				
7				
6				
5				
4				
3				
2				
1				

Graphing

Directions: Look at the graph below. Then answer the questions.

	hot dog	hamburger	pizza	chicken
10				
9				
8			▒	
7			▒	
6	■		▒	■
5	■		▒	■
4	■	▒	▒	■
3	■	▒	▒	■
2	■	▒	▒	■
1	■	▒	▒	■

hot dog   **hamburger**   **pizza**   **chicken**

Name _____

Graphing

◆ How many people like hot dogs best? _____

◆ How many people like pizza best? _____

◆ How many people like chicken best? _____

◆ Which food do most people like best? _____

◆ Which two foods do the same number of people like best?

_____ and _____

◆ Which food do the fewest number of people like best?

_____

Graphing

Directions: Count the pets in the window. Then color one box for each animal on the graph below.

Page 8

Number Recognition

Directions: Write the numbers 1–10. Color the bear.

Page 9

Zero

Directions: Color the tank to show that it has 0 fish. Color the tanks that have 0 fish.

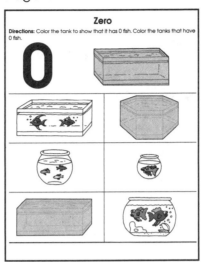

Page 10

One and Two

Directions: Count how many cars are on each track. Circle the number that shows how many.

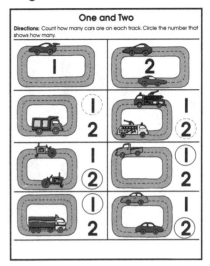

Page 11

Three

Directions: Color the 3 kittens in the basket. Color 3 animals in each group.

Page 12

Four

Directions: Color the 4 crayons. Count how many. Circle the correct number.

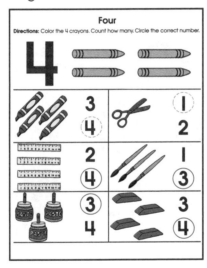

Page 13

Five

Directions: Color the 5 party hats. Color and circle the groups that have 5.

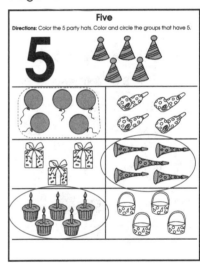

Page 14

Review Numbers 1–5

Directions: Look at the picture. Read the questions. Circle the correct number.

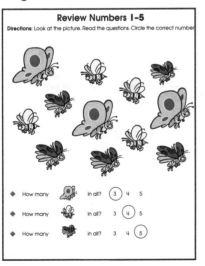

Page 15

Review Numbers 1–5

Directions: Draw a line from the number to the group that matches it.

Page 16

Six

Directions: Look at the number 6. Count the teddy bears. Trace the circle to show this is a group of 6. Circle the group if it shows 6.

Summer Link Super Edition Grade 1

Page 17

Review Numbers 1–6

Directions: Count each group of blocks. Trace each number. Count each group of blocks below. Write the number.

Page 18

Seven

Directions: Look at the number 7. Count how many bees. Color the 7 bees. Count how many. Circle the number.

Page 19

Eight

Directions: Look at the number 8. Count the envelopes. Trace the circle to show this is a group of 8. Circle the group if it shows 8.

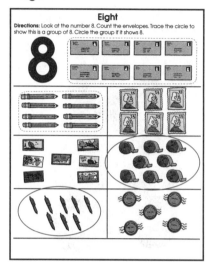

Page 20

Nine

Directions: Look at the number 9. Circle 9 cars. Circle the signs to show the number.

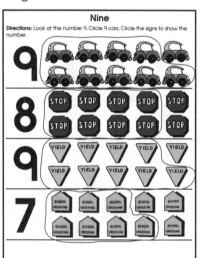

Page 21

Ten

Directions: Look at the number 10. Trace the circle to show this is a group of 10. Circle each group of 10 objects.

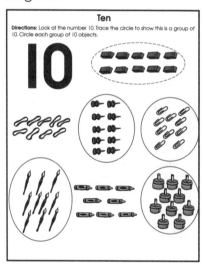

Page 22

Nine and Ten

Directions: Count and write the number in each box. Circle the groups of 9. Color the groups of 10.

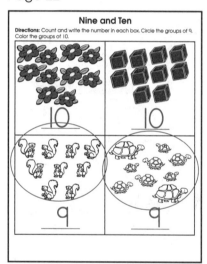

Page 23

Review Numbers 7–10

Directions: Count each group of balloons. Trace each number. Count each group of balloons below. Write the number.

Page 24

Eleven and Twelve

Directions: Trace and write the numbers 11 and 12. Count and write the numbers.

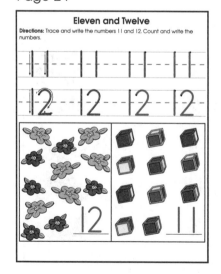

Page 25

Eleven and Twelve

Directions: Draw flowers to show the number in each box.

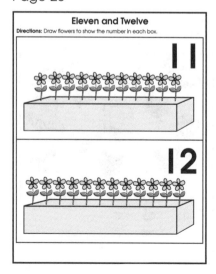

Page 26

Review Numbers 1–12

Directions: Count the number of colored squares. Then write the correct number.

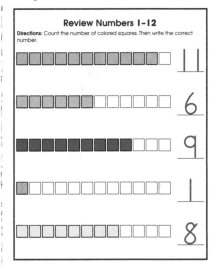

11

6

9

1

8

Page 27

Thirteen

Directions: Trace and write the number 13. Complete each puzzle by writing or drawing the missing number of flowers.

13

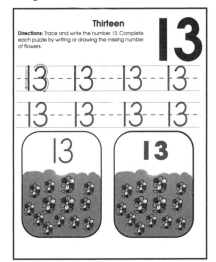

13 13 13 13
13 13 13 13

13   13

Page 28

Fourteen

Directions: Trace and write the number 14. Connect the dots. Color the picture. What is it?

14

14 14 14 14
14 14 14 14

Page 29

Fifteen

Directions: Trace and write the number 15. Write the missing pool ball numbers.

15

15 15 15 15
15 15 15 15

Page 30

Sixteen

Directions: Trace and write the number 16. Draw eight legs on each spider.

16

16 16 16 16
16 16 16 16

How many legs are there in all? _____ 16

Page 31

Seventeen

Directions: Trace and write the number 17. Circle each group of 17 things. Color the dog.

17

17 17 17 17
17 17 17 17

Page 32

Eighteen

Directions: Trace and write the number 18. Help Filbert Fish find his way to the top. Write the numbers 1–18 in each bubble along the way.

18

18 18 18 18
18 18 18 18

Page 33

Nineteen

Directions: Trace and write the number 19. Circle the numbers 1–19 in the picture.

19

19 19 19 19
19 19 19 19

Page 34

Twenty

Directions: Trace and write the number 20. Connect the dots to find the hidden picture. What is it?

20

20 20 20
20 20 20

Summer Link Super Edition Grade 1

Page 35

Number Recognition

Directions: Count the number of objects in each group. Draw a line to the correct number.

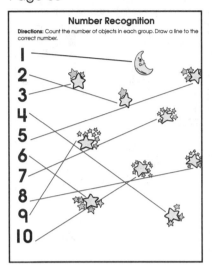

1
2
3
4
5
6
7
8
9
10

Page 36

Number Words

Directions: Number the buildings from one to six.

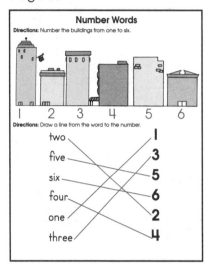

1 2 3 4 5 6

Directions: Draw a line from the word to the number.

two — 1
five — 3
six — 5
four — 6
one — 2
three — 4

Page 37

Number Words

Directions: Number the buildings from five to ten.

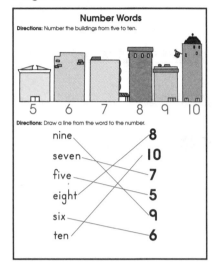

5 6 7 8 9 10

Directions: Draw a line from the word to the number.

nine — 8
seven — 10
five — 7
eight — 5
six — 9
ten — 6

Page 38

Sequencing Numbers

Sequencing is putting numbers in the correct order.

1, 2, 3, 4, 5, 6, 7, 8, 9, 10

Directions: Write the missing numbers.

Example: 4, _5_ , 6

3, _4_ ,5   7, _8_ ,9   8, _9_ ,10
6, _7_ ,8   _2_ ,3, 4   _4_ ,5, 6
5, 6, _7_   _5_ ,6, 7   _2_ ,3, 4
_3_ ,4, 5   _6_ ,7, 8   5, _6_ ,7
2, 3, _4_   1, 2, _3_   7, 8, _9_
2, _3_ ,4   _1_ ,2, 3   4, _5_ ,6
6, 7, _8_   3, 4, _5_   1, _2_ ,3
7, 8, _9_   _2_ ,3, 4   _8_ ,9, 10

Page 39

Review

Directions: Count the objects and write the number.

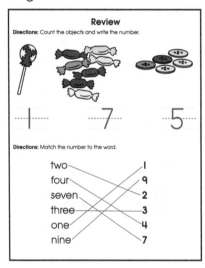

- - - 1 - - -   - - - 7 - - -   - - - 5 - - -

Directions: Match the number to the word.

two — 1
four — 9
seven — 2
three — 3
one — 4
nine — 7

Page 40

Ordinal Numbers

Ordinal numbers are used to indicate order in a series, such as **first, second,** or **third.**

Directions: Draw a line to the picture that goes with the ordinal number in the left column.

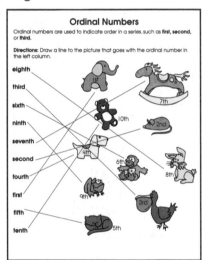

eighth
third
sixth
ninth
seventh
second
fourth
first
fifth
tenth

Page 41

Ordinal Numbers

Directions: Color the first leaf red. Circle the third leaf.

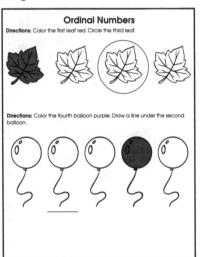

Directions: Color the fourth balloon purple. Draw a line under the second balloon.

Page 42

Orderly Ordinals

Directions: Write each word on the correct line to put the words in order.

| second | fifth | seventh | first | tenth |
| third | eighth | sixth | fourth | ninth |

1. first   6. sixth
2. second   7. seventh
3. third   8. eighth
4. fourth   9. ninth
5. fifth   10. tenth

Directions: Which picture is circled in each row? Underline the word that tells the correct number.

third <u>fourth</u>
fourth sixth
first <u>ninth</u>
<u>third</u> fifth
<u>fifth</u> sixth
<u>second</u> third

Page 43

One for Each

Directions: Each circus seal needs one ball. Draw a ball for each seal.

Page 44

More

Directions: Circle the group in each box that has more.

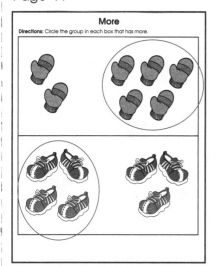

Page 45

More

Directions: Trace the lines to match the rows of mittens one-to-one. Circle the 6 to show that 6 is more than 4. Match the objects one-to-one. Circle the number that is more.

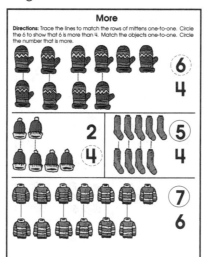

Page 46

Less

Directions: Circle the group in each box that has less.

Page 47

Less

Directions: Trace the lines to match the fish one-to-one. Circle the 4 to show that 4 is less than 6. Match the objects one-to-one. Circle the number that is less.

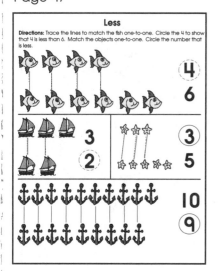

Page 48

Addition 1, 2

Addition means "putting together" or adding two or more numbers to find the sum. "+" is a plus sign. It means to add the 2 numbers. "=" is an equals sign. It tells how much they are together.

Directions: Count the cats and tell how many.

Page 49

Addition

Directions: Count the shapes and write the numbers below to tell how many in all.

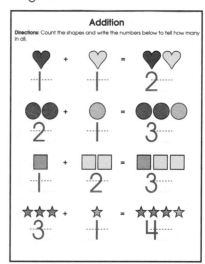

Page 50

Picture Problems: Addition

Directions: Solve the number problem under each picture.

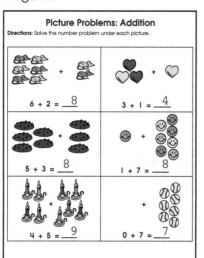

Page 51

How Many in All?

Directions: Count the number in each group and write the number on the line. Then, add the groups together and write the sum.

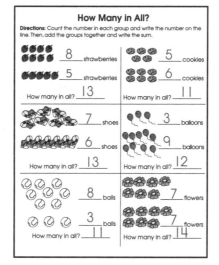

Page 52

Subtraction 1, 2, 3

Subtraction means "taking away" or subtracting one number from another. "-" is a minus sign. It means to subtract the second number from the first.

Directions: Practice writing the numbers and then subtract. Draw dots and cross them out, if needed.

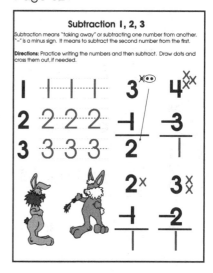

93

Summer Link Super Edition Grade 1

Page 53

Picture Problems: Subtraction

Directions: Solve the number problem under each picture.

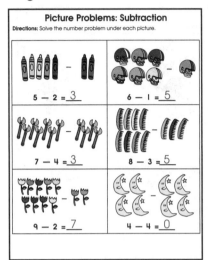

$5 - 2 = \underline{3}$ $6 - 1 = \underline{5}$

$7 - 4 = \underline{3}$ $8 - 3 = \underline{5}$

$9 - 2 = \underline{7}$ $4 - 4 = \underline{0}$

Page 54

Picture Problems: Addition and Subtraction

Directions: Solve the number problem under each picture.

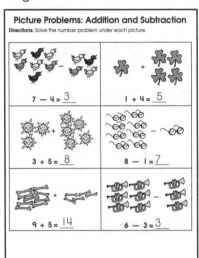

$7 - 4 = \underline{3}$ $1 + 4 = \underline{5}$

$3 + 5 = \underline{8}$ $8 - 1 = \underline{7}$

$9 + 5 = \underline{14}$ $6 - 3 = \underline{3}$

Page 55

Review: Addition and Subtraction

Directions: Solve the number problem under each picture. Write + or – to show if you should add or subtract.

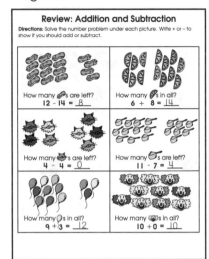

How many 🥜s are left?   How many 🍊s in all?
$12 - 14 = \underline{8}$ $6 + 8 = \underline{14}$

How many 🐱s are left?   How many 🥑s are left?
$4 - 4 = \underline{0}$ $11 - 7 = \underline{4}$

How many 🎈s in all?   How many 🤡s in all?
$9 + 3 = \underline{12}$ $10 + 0 = \underline{10}$

Page 56

Addition and Subtraction

Directions: Solve the problems. Remember, addition means "putting together" or adding two or more numbers to find the sum. Subtraction means "taking away" or subtracting one number from another.

$1 + 3 = \underline{4}$ $4 - 3 = \underline{1}$ $4 + 5 = \underline{9}$

$6 + 1 = \underline{7}$ $7 - 2 = \underline{5}$ $8 - 4 = \underline{4}$

$9 - 1 = \underline{8}$ $10 - 3 = \underline{7}$

$5 - 2 = \underline{3}$ $6 + 3 = \underline{9}$

$8 + 2 = \underline{10}$ $5 + 5 = \underline{10}$

Page 57

Color Fruit

Directions: Solve the addition and subtraction sentences below. Use the code to color the fruit.

3 — yellow   5 — orange   7 — yellow   9 — red
4 — red   6 — purple   8 — green   10 — brown

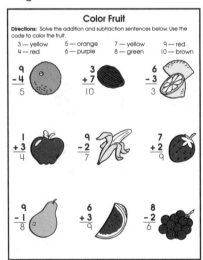

$\begin{array}{r} 9 \\ -4 \\ \hline 5 \end{array}$ $\begin{array}{r} 3 \\ +7 \\ \hline 10 \end{array}$ $\begin{array}{r} 6 \\ -3 \\ \hline 3 \end{array}$

$\begin{array}{r} 1 \\ +3 \\ \hline 4 \end{array}$ $\begin{array}{r} 9 \\ -2 \\ \hline 7 \end{array}$ $\begin{array}{r} 7 \\ +2 \\ \hline 9 \end{array}$

$\begin{array}{r} 9 \\ -1 \\ \hline 8 \end{array}$ $\begin{array}{r} 6 \\ +3 \\ \hline 9 \end{array}$ $\begin{array}{r} 8 \\ -2 \\ \hline 6 \end{array}$

Page 58

Time

Directions: Trace the numbers 1-12 in order on the clock.

Hickory Dickory Dock,
The mouse ran up the clock.
The clock struck one and down he ran.
Hickory Dickory Dock.

Page 59

Time

Directions: Write the time that is on each clock.

Example:

$\underline{2}$ o'clock

$\underline{3}$ o'clock

$\underline{9}$ o'clock

$\underline{6}$ o'clock

Page 60

Time

Directions: Write the time that is on each clock.

$\underline{10}$ o'clock

$\underline{11}$ o'clock

$\underline{7}$ o'clock

$\underline{8}$ o'clock

Page 61

Pennies

Directions: A penny is worth 1¢. It is brown. Circle the correct amount of money in each row below.

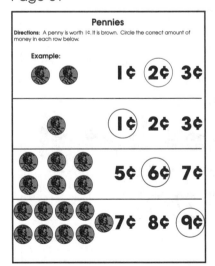

Example:

1¢   (2¢)   3¢

(1¢)   2¢   3¢

5¢   (6¢)   7¢

7¢   8¢   (9¢)

Page 62

Pennies

Directions: Circle the correct amount of money in each row below.

🪙🪙🪙🪙 2¢ 3¢ (4¢)

🪙🪙🪙 1¢ 2¢ (3¢)

🪙🪙🪙🪙🪙 4¢ (5¢) 6¢

🪙🪙🪙🪙🪙🪙🪙🪙 7¢ (8¢) 9¢

Page 63

Nickels

Directions: A nickel is worth 5¢. It is silver. Circle the correct amount of money in each row below.

Example:

🪙 = 🪙🪙🪙🪙🪙
5¢   5¢

🪙🪙🪙🪙🪙 4¢ (5¢) 6¢

🪙🪙 1¢ (2¢) 3¢

🪙 (1¢) 2¢ 3¢

Page 64

Nickels

Directions: Circle the correct amount of money in each row below.

🪙🪙🪙🪙 3¢ (4¢) 5¢

🪙 4¢ (5¢) 6¢

🪙🪙🪙 (3¢) 4¢ 5¢

🪙🪙 4¢ 5¢ (6¢)

Page 65

Dimes

Directions: A dime is worth 10¢. It is silver. Circle the correct amount of money in each row below.

Example:

🪙 = 🪙 = 🪙🪙🪙🪙🪙🪙🪙🪙🪙🪙
10¢   10¢   10¢

🪙 1¢ (5¢) 10¢

🪙🪙 5¢ 7¢ (10¢)

🪙 8¢ 9¢ (10¢)

Page 66

Dimes

Directions: Circle the correct amount of money in each row below.

🪙🪙🪙 2¢ (3¢) 4¢

🪙🪙🪙🪙🪙🪙🪙 5¢ 6¢ (7¢)

🪙🪙🪙🪙🪙 8¢ (9¢) 10¢

🪙🪙 9¢ 10¢ (11¢)

Page 67

Review Money

Directions: Match the price of each thing to the correct amount of money.

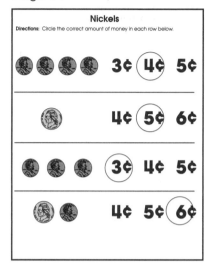

Page 68

Review Money

Directions: Match the coins to the correct amount of money.

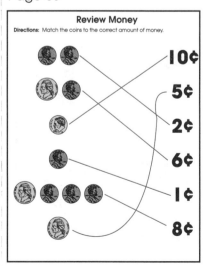

10¢

5¢

2¢

6¢

1¢

8¢

Page 69

Shapes: Square

A square is a figure with four corners and four sides of the same length. This is a square □.

Directions: Find the squares and circle them.

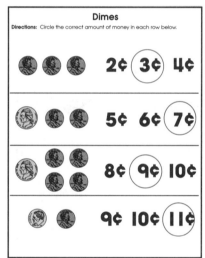

Directions: Trace the word. Write the word.

square   square

Page 70

Shapes: Circle

A circle is a figure that is round. This is a circle ○.

Directions: Find the circles and put a square around them.

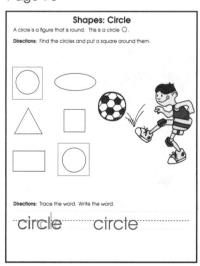

Directions: Trace the word. Write the word.

circle   circle

Page 71

Shapes: Square and Circle

Directions: Practice drawing squares. Trace the samples and make four of your own.

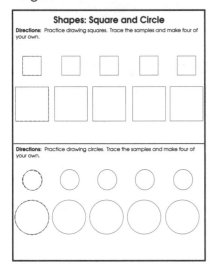

Directions: Practice drawing circles. Trace the samples and make four of your own.

Page 72

Shapes: Triangle

A triangle is a figure with three corners and three sides.

This is a triangle △.

Directions: Find the triangles and put a circle around them.

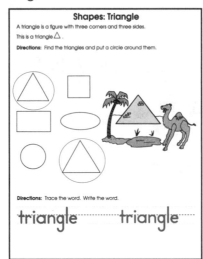

Directions: Trace the word. Write the word.

triangle   triangle

Page 73

Shapes: Rectangle

A rectangle is a figure with four corners and four sides. Sides opposite each other are the same length.

This is a rectangle □.

Directions: Find the rectangles and put a circle around them.

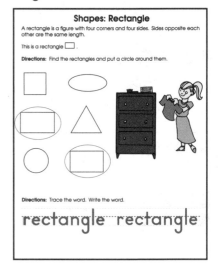

Directions: Trace the word. Write the word.

rectangle rectangle

Page 74

Shapes: Triangle and Rectangle

Directions: Practice drawing triangles. Trace the samples and make four of your own.

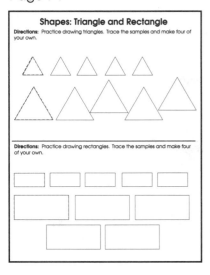

Directions: Practice drawing rectangles. Trace the samples and make four of your own.

Page 75

Shapes: Oval and Diamond

An oval is an egg-shaped figure. A diamond is a figure with four sides of the same length. Its corners form points at the top, sides, and bottom.

This is an oval ◯.   This is a diamond ◇.

Directions: Color the ovals red. Color the diamonds blue.

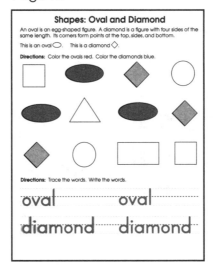

Directions: Trace the words. Write the words.

oval   oval
diamond   diamond

Page 76

Shapes: Oval and Diamond

Directions: Practice drawing ovals. Trace the samples and make four of your own.

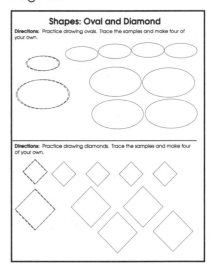

Directions: Practice drawing diamonds. Trace the samples and make four of your own.

Page 77

Animal Shapes

Directions: Color: squares — green   rectangles — yellow
circles — red   triangles — blue

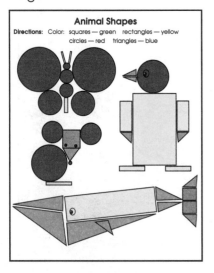

Page 78

Classifying: Shapes

Mary and Rudy are taking a trip into space. Help them find the stars, moons, circles, and diamonds.

Directions: Color the shapes.
Use yellow for ☆s.   Use blue for ☾s.
Use red for ◯s.   Use purple for ◇s.

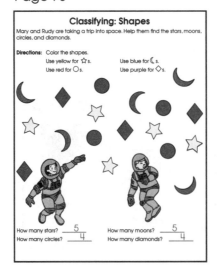

How many stars? __5__   How many moons? __5__
How many circles? __4__   How many diamonds? __4__

Page 79

Same Shape

Directions: Look at the round shapes. They are all the same shape. Draw a line from each shape in the bottom row to the box with the same shape.

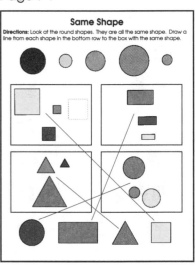

Page 80

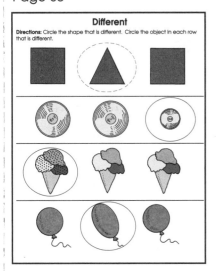

Different

Directions: Circle the shape that is different. Circle the object in each row that is different.

Page 81

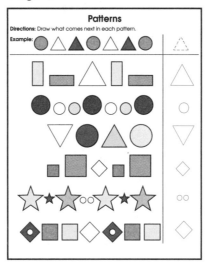

Patterns

Directions: Draw what comes next in each pattern.

Example:

Page 82

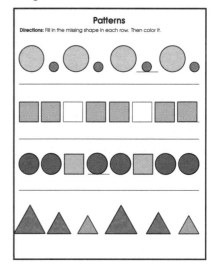

Patterns

Directions: Fill in the missing shape in each row. Then color it.

Page 83

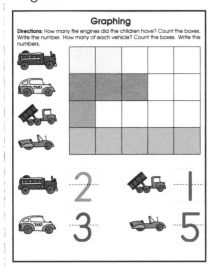

Graphing

Directions: How many fire engines did the children have? Count the boxes. Write the number. How many of each vehicle? Count the boxes. Write the numbers.

2 |
3   5

Page 84

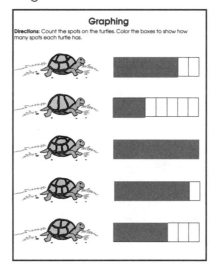

Graphing

Directions: Count the spots on the turtles. Color the boxes to show how many spots each turtle has.

Page 85

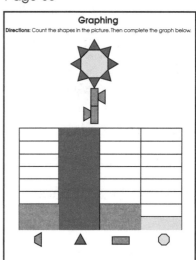

Graphing

Directions: Count the shapes in the picture. Then complete the graph below.

Page 87

Graphing

◆ How many people like hot dogs best? _____ 6

◆ How many people like pizza best? _____ 8

◆ How many people like chicken best? _____ 6

◆ Which food do most people like best? pizza

◆ Which two foods do the same number of people like best?
hot dogs and chicken

◆ Which food do the fewest number of people like best?
hamburgers

Page 88

Graphing

Directions: Count the pets in the window. Then color one box for each animal on the graph below.

Developmental Skills for First Grade Math Success

This checklist is designed to help you assess your child's progress in the following kindergarten skills. You may want to add to or adapt this checklist to fit your child's abilities.

Basic Skills

Names basic colors _____

Names simple shapes _____

Identifies opposites _____

Understands positional concepts _____

Names days of the week in order _____

Mathematics Readiness

Counts objects to 20 _____

Writes numbers to 20 _____

Identifies numbers to 20 in random order _____

Rote counts to 100 _____

Counts by 10's to 100 _____

Uses ordinal numbers_____

Reads a graph_____

Identifies and continues established patterns _____

Math Worksheet

Math Worksheet

Math Worksheet

Math Worksheet

Math Worksheet

Math Worksheet

Math Worksheet

This page intentionally left blank.

READING

This page intentionally left blank.

All About Me!

This book belongs to

_ _ _ _ _ _ _ _ _ _ _ _ _ _ _ _ _ _ _ ▪

I live at

_ _ _ _ _ _ _ _ _ _ _ _ _ _ _ _ _ _ _ ▪

The city I live in is

_ _ _ _ _ _ _ _ _ _ _ _ _ _ _ _ _ _ _ ▪

The state I live in is

_ _ _ _ _ _ _ _ _ _ _ _ _ _ _ _ _ _ _ ▪

My phone number is

_ _ _ _ _ _ _ _ _ _ _ _ _ _ _ _ _ _ _ ▪

Recommended Reading
Summer Before Grade 1

- **Anno's Counting House**   Mitsuma Anno

- **Boomer Goes to School**   Constance McGeorge

- **Cam Jansen and the Birthday Mystery**   David Adler

- **Count-A-Saurus**   Nancy Blumenthal

- **Curious George**   H.A. Rey

- **Elmer**   David McKee

- **Franklin Plays the Game**   Paulette Bourgeois

- **The Giving Tree**   Shel Silverstein

- **The Great Kapok Tree**   Lynne Cherry

- **Have You Seen My Cat?**   Eric Carle

- **I Know About Counting**   Henry Pluckrose

- **I Love Colors**   Stan and Jan Berenstain

- **The Little Red Hen** Paul Galdone

- **Numbers at Play: A Counting Book** Charles Sullivan

- **Omar's Quilt** Paulette Bourgeois

- **Peter Rabbit's 1 2 3** Beatrix Potter

- **Pumpkin, Pumpkin** Jean Titherington

- **Q Is For Duck** Mary Elting and
  Michael Folsom

- **The Quilt Keeping** Patricia Polacco

- **Somebody and the Three Blairs** Marilyn Tolhurst

- **Ten Apples Up On Top** Theo LeSeig

- **The Wheels On The Bus** Harriet Ziefert

Zebra A to Z

Directions: Help the Zebra find his way back to the zoo.
Color the boxes ☐ from **A** to **Z**.

Alphabet X-Ray

Directions: Trace all the letters in the X-ray. **Color** the picture.

ABC Order Dot-to-Dot

Directions: ABC order is the order in which letters come in the alphabet. Draw a line to connect the dots. Follow the letters in **abc** order. Then color the picture.

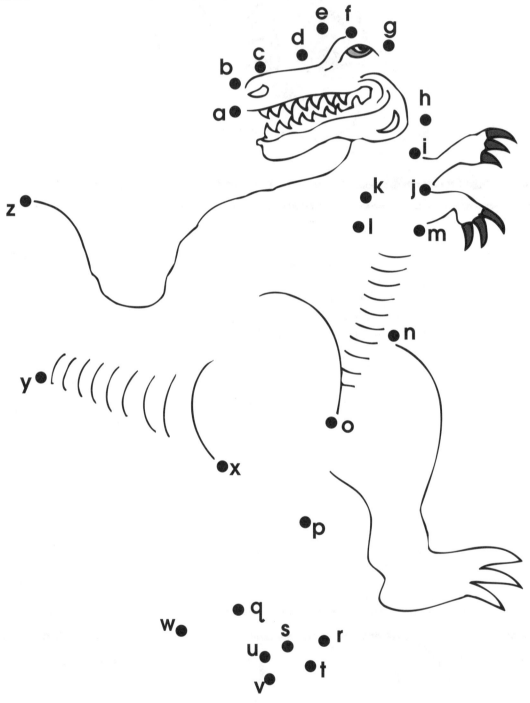

ABC Order

Directions: Put the words in abc order. Circle the first letter of each word. Then write 1, 2, 3, 4, 5, or 6 on the line next to each animal's name.

skunk _____

dog _____

butterfly _____

zebra _____

tiger _____

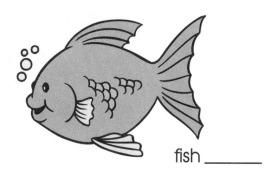

fish _____

Name _____

ABC Order

Directions: Put each group of words in ABC order by numbering them 1, 2, 3.

Example:

cold	**w**arm	**h**ot
1	3	2
small	**b**ig	**c**ute
_____	_____	_____

Uppercase Letters

Directions: Write the missing uppercase letters to complete the alphabet.

Lowercase Letters

Directions: Write the missing lowercase letters to the complete the alphabet.

Name _____

Uppercase Hidden Letters

Directions: Circle each hidden letter of the alphabet below.

Name _____

Gum Ball Dot-to-Dot

Directions: Connect the dots from **A–Z.**
Color the gum balls your favorite colors.

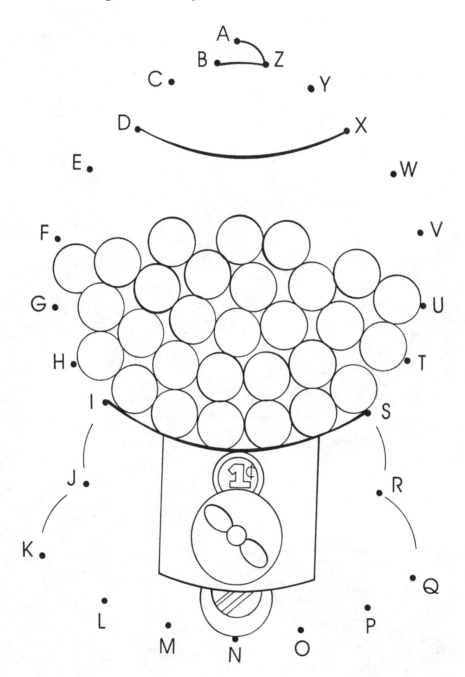

Alphabet Review

Directions: Trace the UPPER-CASE letters.
Write the missing UPPER-CASE letters.

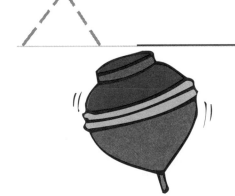

Letter Match

Directions: Draw a line to match each UPPER-CASE letter with the correct lower-case letter.

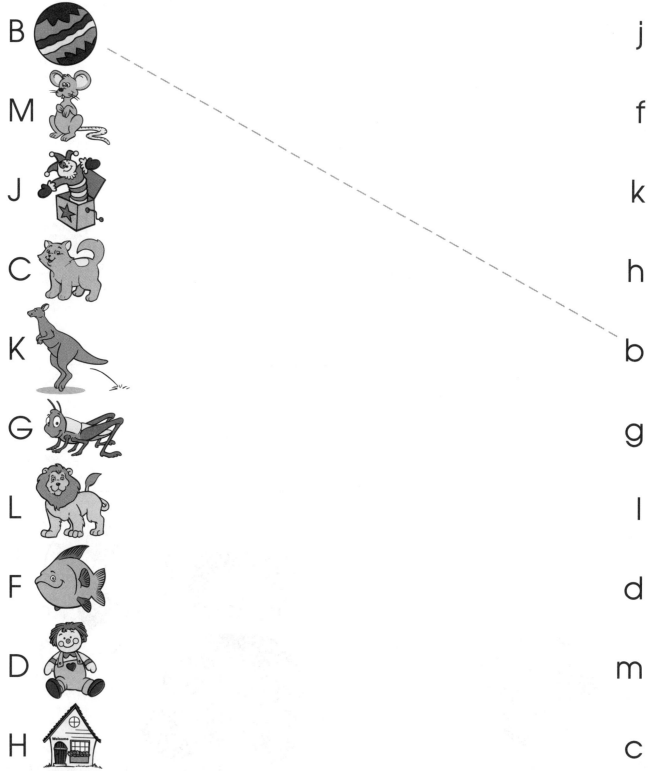

B   j

M   f

J   k

C   h

K   b

G   g

L   l

F   d

D   m

H   c

Name _____

A-Z Penguin

Directions: Draw a line from A-Z to show the way to Penguin's house.

Writing Your Name

Directions: Write your name. Draw a picture of yourself doing something
you like.

Address Dot-to-Dot

Directions: Connect the dots in ABC order. What did you find?

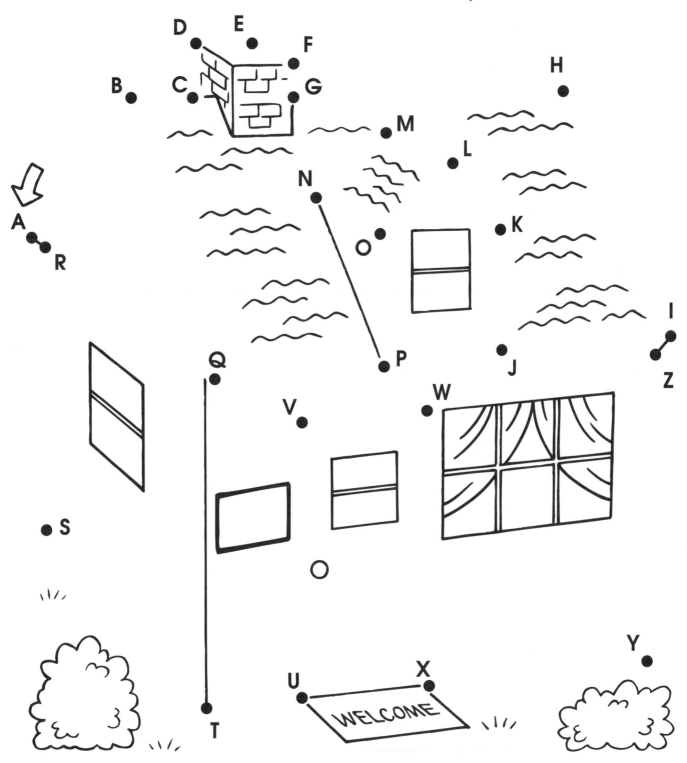

Write your house or apartment number on the house.

Writing Your Address

Directions: Write your address. Draw a picture to show where you live.

_____

- - - - - - - - - - - - - - - - - - - -

_____

- - - - - - - - - - - - - - - - - - - -

_____

Name _____

Beginning Sound Game

Directions: Cut out the letters and pictures below and on pages 23–27. Mix them up and turn them over to match the beginning sound with its picture.

Aa	Bb	Cc
Dd	Ee	Ff
Gg	Hh	Ii
Jj	Kk	Ll
Mm	Nn	Oo

This page was left intentionally blank for cutting activity on previous page.

Beginning Sound Game

Pp	Qq	Rr
Ss	Tt	Uu
Vv	Ww	Xx
Yy	Zz	

This page was left intentionally
blank for cutting activity on
previous page.

Beginning Sound Game

This page was left intentionally
blank for cutting activity on
previous page.

Beginning Sound Game

Summer Link Super Edition Grade 1

This page was left intentionally blank for cutting activity on previous page.

Beginning Sounds

Directions: Write the beginning sound for each picure. **Color** the pictures.

Summer Link Super Edition Grade 1

Ending Sounds

Directions: Circle the ending sound for each picure.

l	r	t	x
l	r	t	x
l	r	t	x
l	r	t	x
l	r	t	x
l	r	t	x
l	r	t	x
l	r	t	x
l	r	t	x
l	r	t	x
l	r	t	x
l	r	t	x

Name _____

Beginning Consonants

Beginning consonants are the sounds that come at the beginning of words. Consonants are the letters b, c, d, f, g, h, j, k, l, m, n, p, q, r, s, t, v, w, x, y, and z.

Directions: Say the name of each letter. Say the sound each letter makes. Circle the letters that make the beginning sound for each picture.

Bb   Cc   Dd   Ff

Bb Dd   Ff Cc   Cc Dd   Ff Bb

Bb Dd   Ff Cc   Cc Dd   Ff Bb

    Summer Link Super Edition Grade 1

Name _____

Beginning Consonants

Directions: Say the name of each letter. Say the sound each letter makes. Draw a line from each letter to the picture which begins with that sound.

Ff

Dd

Cc

Bb

Dd

Ff

Cc

Bb

Name _____

Beginning Consonants

Directions: Say the name of each letter. Say the sound each letter makes.
Trace the letter pair that makes the beginning sound in each picture.

Gg   Hh   Jj   Kk

Kk   Hh

Gg   Kk

Gg   Hh

Jj   Gg

139   Summer Link Super Edition Grade 1

Beginning Consonants

Directions: Say the name of each letter. Say the sound each letter makes. Draw a line from each letter pair to the picture which begins with that sound.

Gg

Kk

Hh

Jj

Kk

Hh

Jj

Gg

Beginning Consonants

Directions: Say the name of each letter. Say the sound each letter makes. Trace the letters. Then draw a line from each letter pair to the picture which begins with that sound.

Beginning Consonants

Directions: Say the name of each letter. Say the sound each letter makes. Trace the letter pair that makes the beginning sound in each picture.

Ll   Mm   Nn   Pp

Mm   Ll

Mm   Pp

Ll   Nn

Pp   Mm

Name _____

Beginning Consonants

Directions: Say the name of each letter. Say the sound each letter makes. Trace the letter pair in the boxes. Then color the picture which begins with that sound.

Qq   Rr   Ss   Tt

Tt

Qq

Rr

Ss

Beginning Consonants

Directions: Say the name of each letter. Say the sound each letter makes. Draw a line from each letter pair to the picture which begins with that sound.

Qq

Ss

Rr

Tt

Tt

Ss

Rr

Qq

Beginning Consonants

Directions: Say the name of each letter. Say the sound each letter makes. Trace the letters. Then draw a line from each letter pair to the picture which begins with that sound.

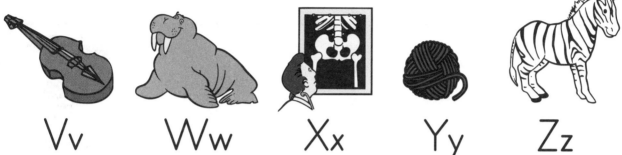

V v   W w   X x   Y y   Z z

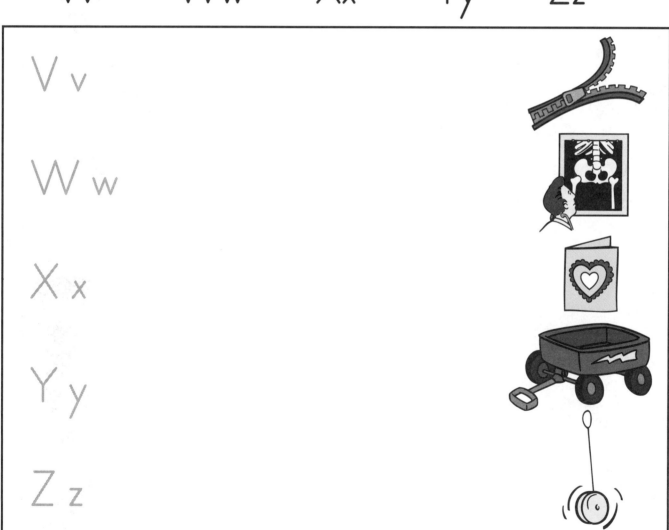

V v

W w

X x

Y y

Z z

Beginning Consonants

Directions: Say the name of each letter. Say the sound each letter makes. Trace the letters. Then draw a line from each letter pair to the picture which begins with that sound.

Vv

Zz

Xx

Yy

Ww

Vv

Zz

Yy

Ww

Xx

Name _____

Beginning Consonants

Directions: Say each picture name. Circle the letter that stands for the beginning sound.

r n	m f	k b
l h	s w	d m
n d	l p	y w

Beginning Consonants

Directions: Say each picture name. Circle the beginning sound.

t p	n c	b t
b c	t p	c b
c t	b p	p n

Beginning Consonants

Directions: Look at the picture in each box. Color the pictures in that row with the same beginning sound.

Ending Consonant Blends

Directions: Draw a line from the picture to the blend that ends the word.

lf

lk

sk

st

Ending Consonant Blends

Directions: Every juke box has a word ending and a list of letters. Add each of the letters to the word ending to make rhyming words.

___and

b _____
h _____
l _____
s _____

___ent

b _____
d _____
t _____
w _____

___ump

b _____
d _____
j _____
p _____

___ink

p _____
s _____
l _____
th _____

___ing

r _____
s _____
st _____
k _____

___ank

b _____
r _____
s _____
t _____

151   Summer Link Super Edition Grade 1

Ending Consonant Sounds

Directions: Look at the picture in each box. Circle the ending sound for each picture.

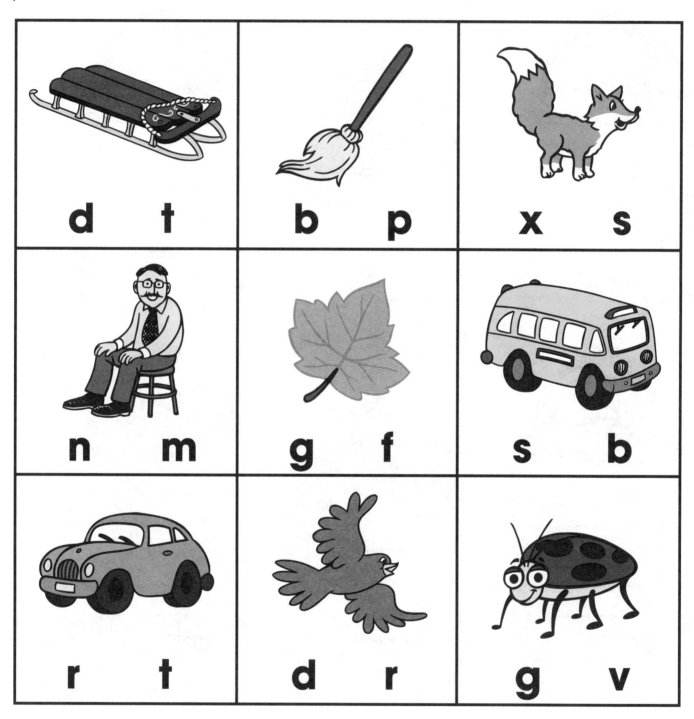

d t	b p	x s
n m	**g f**	**s b**
r t	**d r**	**g v**

Ending Consonant Sounds

Directions: Say each picture name. Fill in the circle next to the ending sound.

○ t ○ p	○ n ○ b	○ b ○ t
○ n ○ p	○ p ○ b	○ p ○ t
○ b ○ p	○ n ○ p	○ t ○ n

Summer Link Super Edition Grade 1

Name _____

Short Vowels

Vowels are the letters **a, e, i, o,** and **u.** Short **a** is the sound you hear in **ant.** Short **e** is the sound you hear in **elephant.** Short **i** is the sound you hear in **igloo.** Short **o** is the sound you hear in **octopus.** Short **u** is the sound you hear in **umbrella.**

Directions: Say the short vowel sound at the beginning of each row. Say the name of each picture. Then color the pictures which have the same short vowel sounds as that letter.

ĕ

ĭ

ŏ

ŭ

Vowels

Directions: In each box are three pictures. The words that name the pictures have missing letters. Write **a, e, i, o,** or **u** to finish the words.

p ____ n

p ____ n

p ____ n

b ____ g

b ____ g

b ____ g

c ____ t

c ____ t

c ____ t

h ____ t

h ____ t

h ____ t

Long Vowels

Vowels are the letters **a, e, i, o,** and **u.** Long vowel sounds say their own names. Long **a** is the sound you hear in **hay.** Long **e** is the sound you hear in **me.** Long **i** is the sound you hear in **pie.** Long **o** is the sound you hear in no. Long **u** is the sound you hear in **cute.**

Directions: Say the long vowel sound at the beginning of each row. Say the name of each picture. Color the pictures in each row that have the same long vowel sound as that letter.

Long Vowels

Directions: Write **a, e, i, o,** or **u** in each blank to finish the word. Draw a line from the word to the picture.

c _____ ke

r _____ se

k _____ te

f _____ t

m _____ le

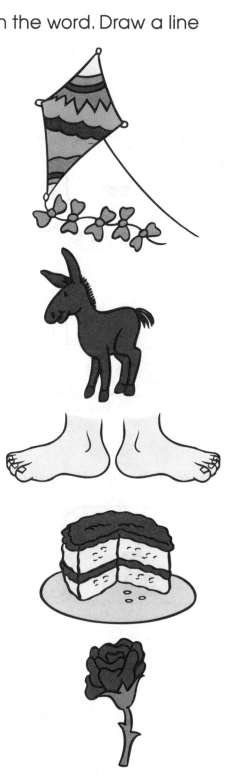

Name _____

Vowels: A

Directions: Each train has a group of pictures. Write the word that names the pictures. Read your rhyming words.

These trains use the short **a** sound like in the word cat:

These trains use the long **a** sound like in the word lake:

Name _____

Vowels: A

Directions: Say the name of each picture. If it has the short **a** sound, color it **red.** If it has the long **a** sound, color it **yellow.**

ă

ā

Summer Link Super Edition Grade 1

Vowels: E

Directions: Short **e** sounds like the e in hen. Long **e** sounds like the **e** in **bee**. Look at the pictures. If the word has a short **e** sound, draw a line to the **hen** with your **red** crayon. If the word has a long **e** sound, draw a line to the **bee** with your **green** crayon.

hen

bee

Vowels: E

Directions: Say the name of each picture. Circle the pictures which have the short **e** sound. Draw a triangle around the pictures which have the long **e** sound.

ĕ

ē

   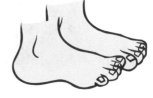

Vowels: I

Directions: Short **i** sounds like the **i** in pig. Long **i** sounds like the **i** in kite. Draw a circle around the words with the short **i** sound. Draw an **X** on the words with the long **i** sound.

five

pig

pin

slide

kite

lid

tie

bib

pie

Vowels: I

Directions: Say the name of each picture. If it has the short **i** sound, color it **yellow.** If it has the long **i** sound, color it **red.**

ĭ

ī

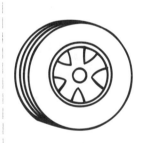

Name _____

Vowels: O

Directions: The short **o** sounds like the **o** in dog. Long **o** sounds like the **o** in rope. Draw a line from the picure to the word that names it. Draw a circle around the word if it has a short **o** sound.

hot dog

fox

blocks

rose

boat

Name _____

Vowels: O

Directions: Say the name of each picture. If the picture has the long **o** sound, write a **green L** on the blank. If the picture has the short **o** sound, write a **red S** on the blank.

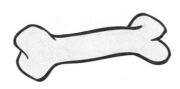

_____ _____

_____ _____ _____

_____ _____ _____

Vowels: U

Directions: The short **u** sounds like the **u** in bug. The long **u** sounds like the **u** in blue. Draw a circle around the words with short **u**. Draw an **X** on the words with long **u**.

rug

cup

music

tub

suit

glue

bug

puppy

gum

Vowels: U

Directions: Say the name of each picture. If it has the long **u** sound, write a **u** in the **unicorn** column. If it has the short **u** sound, write a **u** in the **umbrella** column.

$\bar{u}$ $\breve{u}$

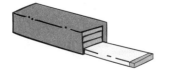

_____   _____

_____   _____

_____   _____

_____   _____

_____   _____

Vowels: E

When you add an **e** to the end of some words, the vowel changes from a short vowel sound to a long vowel sound. The **e** is silent.

Example: rip + **e** = ripe

Directions: Say the word under the first picture in each pair. Then add an **e** to the word under the next picture. Say the new word.

pet   _____

tub   _____

man   _____

kit   _____

pin   _____

cap   _____

Vowels

Directions: Say the name of each picture. Write the letter to complete each word.

_____

c   p

_____

p   g

d   g

b   ll

p   n

b   d

Vowel Maze

Directions: Color your way through the maze by only coloring the vowels. Then write the five vowels below.

START ↓

a	b	m	d	t	g	r
e	m	a	u	o	d	p
o	i	e	k	i	i	e
h	n	c	w	r	n	a
u	o	i	b	o	o	u
a	p	i	e	a	f	k
e	a	c	s	y	l	j

END ↓

___ ___ ___ ___ ___

Nouns

Directions: Draw a line to match each word with its picture.

boy

girl

man

woman

Name _____

Nouns

Directions: Draw a line to match each word with its picture.

ball

apple

bed

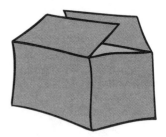

box

Nouns

Directions: Draw a line to match each word with its picture.

cat

flower

car

tree

Name _____

Verbs

Directions: Draw a line to match the action word with the person doing that action.

play

ride

sit

cook

Nouns and Verbs

Directions: Cut out the words below. Glue naming words in the **Nouns** box. Glue action words in the **Verbs** box.

Nouns	Verbs

cut ✂ —

boy   jump   cat   sit

throw   house   swim   fork

This page was left intentionally blank for cutting activity on previous page.

Verbs

Directions: Draw a line to match the action word with the person doing that action.

walk

run

talk

eat

Animal Names

Directions: Fill in the missing letters for each word.

Example:

fr og   fr og

fi _ _   f _ sh

d _ g   _ og

b _ _ d   _ ir _

c _ t   _ a _

Animal Names

Directions: The letters in the name of each animal are mixed up.
Write each word correctly.

Example:

g f o r   frog

t a c

o d g

i f s h

d i b r

Spelling

Directions: Write the word that completes each sentence. Put a **period** at the end of the telling sentences and a **question mark** at the end of the asking sentences.

Example: Does the sun shine on the ___flowers___?

tree	grass	pond	sand	sky

1. The _____ was full of dark clouds☐

2. Can you climb the _____ ☐

3. Did you see the duck in the _____ ☐

4. Is the child playing in the _____ ☐

5. The _____ in the yard was tall☐

Spelling

Some words are opposites. Opposites are things that are different in every way. **Dark** and **light** are opposites.

Directions: Trace the letters to write each word. Then write the word again by yourself.

Example:

new   new

old

big

little

lost

found

Sentences

Sentences begin with capital letters.

Directions: Read the sentences and write them below. Begin each sentence with a capital letter.

The cat is fat.

my dog is big.

----

the boy is sad.

----

bikes are fun!

----

dad can bake.

Word Order Activity

Word order is the order of words in a sentence which makes sense.

Directions: Cut out the words and put them in the correct order. Glue each sentence on another sheet of paper.

I	like	bike.	to	ride	my

hot.	It	is	and	sunny

drink	I	can	water.

My	me.	with	plays	mom

tricks.	do	can	The	dog

you	go	store?	to	the	Can

This page was left intentionally blank for cutting activity on previous page.

People Words

Sometimes we use other words in place of people names. For **boy** or **man,** we can use the word **he.** For **girl** or **woman,** we can use the word **she.** For two or more people, we can use the word **they.**

Directions: Write the words **he, she,** or **they** in these sentences.

Example: The boy likes cookies.    likes cookies.

1. The girl is running fast.   _____ is running fast.

2. The man reads the paper.   _____ reads the paper.

3. The woman has a cold.   _____ has a cold.

4. Two children came to school.   _____ came to school.

Name _____

Rhymes

Directions: Words that have the same ending sounds are called **rhyming** words. Circle the pairs that rhyme.

map	nest		dog	frog

hat   bat   kite   mop

can   fan   rat   pig

Rhyming Pairs

Directions: Look at each pair of words and pictures. Circle the pairs that rhyme.

   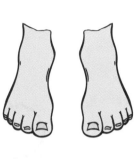

nose   **hose**   **beet**   **feet**

  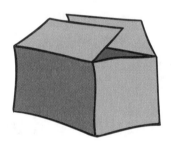 

star   **jar**   **box**   **fox**

dish   **fish**   **cake**   **cap**

Rhymes

Directions: Read the poem. Read the questions. Circle the correct answer.

Jack and Jill went up the hill,
To fetch a pail of water.
Jack fell down and broke his crown,
And Jill came tumbling after.

Who went up the hill?

What were they going to fetch?

Who fell down?

Rhymes

Directions: Read about words that rhyme. Then circle the answers.

Words that rhyme have the same end sounds. **Wing** and **sing** rhyme. **Boy** and **toy** rhyme. **Dime** and **time** rhyme. Can you think of other words that rhyme?

1. Words that rhyme have the same (end letters / end sounds).

> TREE, SEE
> SHOE, BLUE
> KITE, BITE
> MAKE, TAKE
> FLY, BUY

2. Time rhymes with (tree / dime).

Directions: Write one rhyme for each word.

wing

----

boy

----

dime

----

pink

Page 112

Zebra A to Z

Directions: Help the Zebra find his way back to the zoo.
Color the boxes ☐ from **A to Z**.

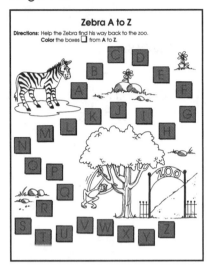

Page 115

ABC Order

Directions: Put the words in abc order. Circle the first letter of each word. Then write 1, 2, 3, 4, 5, or 6 on the line next to each animal's name.

(s)kunk 4
(d)og 2
(b)utterfly 1
(z)ebra 6
(t)iger 5
(f)ish 3

Page 116

ABC Order

Directions: Put each group of words in ABC order by numbering them 1, 2, 3.

Example:

cold	warm	hot
1	3	2

small	big	cute
3	1	2

baby 1
sister 3
family 2
doll 2
truck 3
ball 1
man 3
boy 1
grandma 2

Page 117

Uppercase Letters

Directions: Write the missing uppercase letters to complete the alphabet.

V W X Y Z
U T S R Q P O
H I J K L M N
G F E D C B A

Page 118

Lowercase Letters

Directions: Write the missing lowercase letters to the complete the alphabet.

z y x w v
u t
o p q r s
n m l k j i h
g
a b c d e f

Page 119

Uppercase Hidden Letters

Directions: Circle each hidden letter of the alphabet below.

Page 121

Alphabet Review

Directions: **Trace** the UPPER-CASE letters.
Write the missing UPPER-CASE letters.

A B C D E F
G H I J K L
M N O P Q
R S T U V W
X Y Z

Page 122

Letter Match

Directions: Draw a line to match each UPPER-CASE letter with the correct lower-case letter.

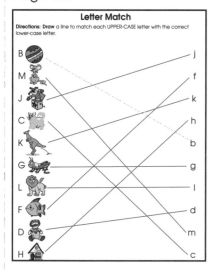

B   j
M   f
J   k
C   h
K   b
G   g
L   l
F   d
D   m
H   c

Page 123

A–Z Penguin

Directions: Draw a line from A–Z to show the way to Penguin's house.

Page 125

Address Dot-to-Dot

Directions: Connect the dots in ABC order. What did you find?

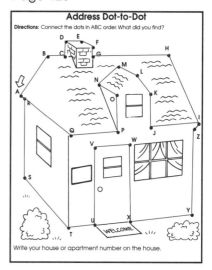

Write your house or apartment number on the house.

Page 135

Beginning Sounds

Directions: Write the beginning sound for each picture. Color the pictures.

t   m
b   w
s   f
l   k
c   e

Page 136

Ending Sounds

Directions: Circle the ending sound for each picure.

Page 137

Beginning Consonants

Beginning consonants are the sounds that come at the beginning of words. Consonants are the letters b, c, d, f, g, h, j, k, l, m, n, p, q, r, s, t, v, w, x, y, and z.

Directions: Say the name of each letter. Say the sound each letter makes. Circle the letters that make the beginning sound for each picture.

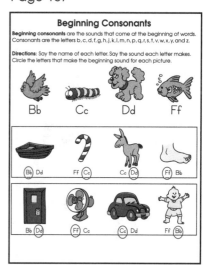

Bb   Cc   Dd   Ff

Page 138

Beginning Consonants

Directions: Say the name of each letter. Say the sound each letter makes. Draw a line from each letter to the picture which begins with that sound.

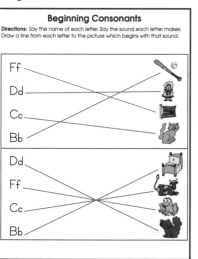

Ff
Dd
Cc
Bb

Dd
Ff
Cc
Bb

Page 139

Beginning Consonants

Directions: Say the name of each letter. Say the sound each letter makes. Trace the letter pair that makes the beginning sound in each picture.

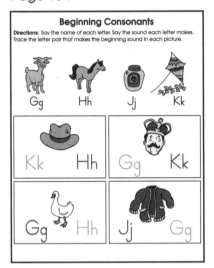

Page 140

Beginning Consonants

Directions: Say the name of each letter. Say the sound each letter makes. Draw a line from each letter pair to the picture which begins with that sound.

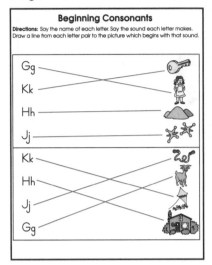

Page 141

Beginning Consonants

Directions: Say the name of each letter. Say the sound each letter makes. Trace the letters. Then draw a line from each letter pair to the picture which begins with that sound.

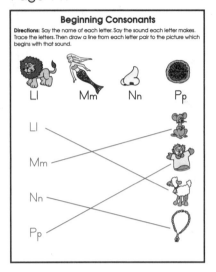

Page 142

Beginning Consonants

Directions: Say the name of each letter. Say the sound each letter makes. Trace the letter pair that makes the beginning sound in each picture.

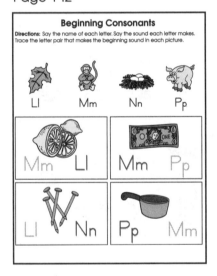

Page 143

Beginning Consonants

Directions: Say the name of each letter. Say the sound each letter makes. Trace the letter pair in the boxes. Then color the picture which begins with that sound.

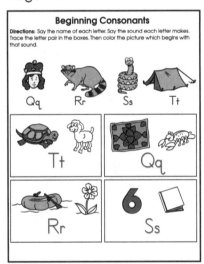

Page 144

Beginning Consonants

Directions: Say the name of each letter. Say the sound each letter makes. Draw a line from each letter pair to the picture which begins with that sound.

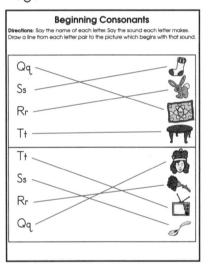

Page 145

Beginning Consonants

Directions: Say the name of each letter. Say the sound each letter makes. Trace the letters. Then draw a line from each letter pair to the picture which begins with that sound.

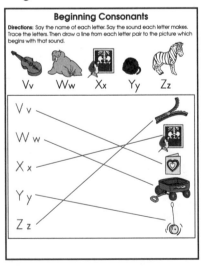

Page 146

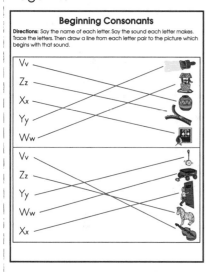

Beginning Consonants

Directions: Say the name of each letter. Say the sound each letter makes. Trace the letters. Then draw a line from each letter pair to the picture which begins with that sound.

Vv
Zz
Xx
Yy
Ww

Vv
Zz
Yy
Ww
Xx

Page 147

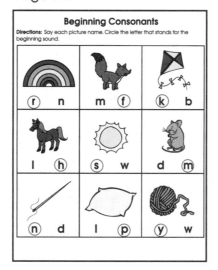

Beginning Consonants

Directions: Say each picture name. Circle the letter that stands for the beginning sound.

(r) n	m (f)	(k) b
l (h)	(s) w	d (m)
(n) d	l (p)	(y) w

Page 148

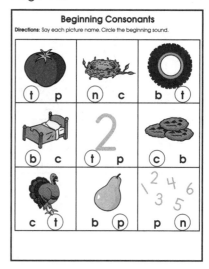

Beginning Consonants

Directions: Say each picture name. Circle the beginning sound.

(t) p	(n) c	b (t)
(b) c	(t) p	(c) b
c (t)	b (p)	p (n)

Page 149

Beginning Consonants

Directions: Look at the picture in each box. Color the pictures in that row with the same beginning sound.

Page 150

Ending Consonant Blends

Directions: Draw a line from the picture to the blend that ends the word.

lf

lk

sk

st

Page 151

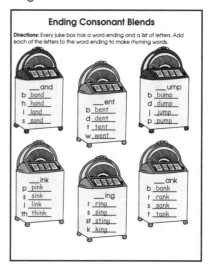

Ending Consonant Blends

Directions: Every juke box has a word ending and a list of letters. Add each of the letters to the word ending to make rhyming words.

___ and
b _band_
h _hand_
l _land_
s _sand_

___ ent
b _bent_
d _dent_
t _tent_
w _went_

___ ump
b _bump_
d _dump_
j _jump_
p _pump_

___ ink
p _pink_
s _sink_
l _link_
th _think_

___ ing
r _ring_
s _sing_
st _sting_
k _king_

___ ank
b _bank_
r _rank_
s _sank_
t _tank_

Page 152

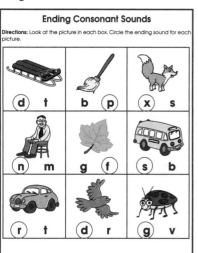

Ending Consonant Sounds

Directions: Look at the picture in each box. Circle the ending sound for each picture.

(d) t	b (p)	(x) s
(n) m	g (f)	(s) b
r t	(d) r	(g) v

Summer Link Super Edition Grade 1

Page 153

Ending Consonant Sounds

Directions: Say each picture name. Fill in the circle next to the ending sound.

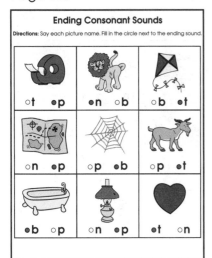

Page 154

Short Vowels

Vowels are the letters **a, e, i, o,** and **u**. Short **a** is the sound you hear in **ant**. Short **e** is the sound you hear in **elephant**. Short **i** is the sound you hear in **igloo**. Short **o** is the sound you hear in **octopus**. Short **u** is the sound you hear in **umbrella**.

Directions: Say the short vowel sound at the beginning of each row. Say the name of each picture. Then color the pictures which have the same short vowel sounds as that letter.

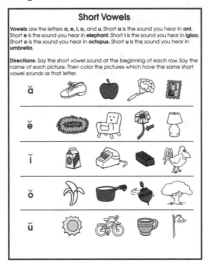

Page 155

Vowels

Directions: In each box are three pictures. The words that name the pictures have missing letters. Write **a, e, i, o,** or **u** to finish the words.

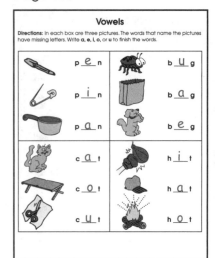

Page 156

Long Vowels

Vowels are the letters **a, e, i, o,** and **u**. Long vowel sounds say their own names. Long **a** is the sound you hear in **hay**. Long **e** is the sound you hear in **me**. Long **i** is the sound you hear in **pie**. Long **o** is the sound you hear in **no**. Long **u** is the sound you hear in **cute**.

Directions: Say the long vowel sound at the beginning of each row. Say the name of each picture. Color the pictures in each row that have the same long vowel sound as that letter.

Page 157

Long Vowels

Directions: Write **a, e, i, o,** or **u** in each blank to finish the word. Draw a line from the word to the picture.

Page 158

Vowels: A

Directions: Each train has a group of pictures. Write the word that names the pictures. Read your rhyming words.

These trains use the short **a** sound like in the word **cat**:

These trains use the long **a** sound like in the word **lake**:

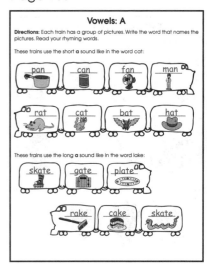

Page 159

Vowels: A

Directions: Say the name of each picture. If it has the short **a** sound, color it **red**. If it has the long **a** sound, color it **yellow**.

Page 160

Vowels: E

Directions: Short **e** sounds like the **e** in hen. Long **e** sounds like the **e** in **bee**. Look at the pictures. If the word has a short **e** sound, draw a line to the **hen** with your **red** crayon. If the word has a long **e** sound, draw a line to the **bee** with your **green** crayon.

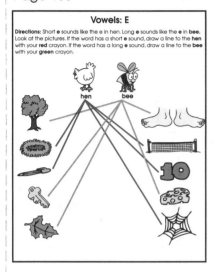

Page 161

Vowels: E

Directions: Say the name of each picture. Circle the pictures which have the short **e** sound. Draw a triangle around the pictures which have the long **e** sound.

Page 162

Vowels: I

Directions: Short **i** sounds like the **i** in pig. Long **i** sounds like the **i** in kite. Draw a circle around the words with the short **i** sound. Draw an **X** on the words with the long **i** sound.

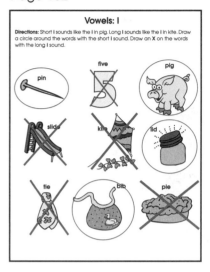

Page 163

Vowels: I

Directions: Say the name of each picture. If it has the short **i** sound, color it **yellow**. If it has the long **i** sound, color it **red**.

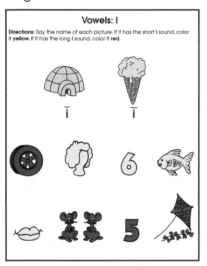

Page 164

Vowels: O

Directions: The short **o** sounds like the **o** in dog. Long **o** sounds like the **o** in rope. Draw a line from the picture to the word that names it. Draw a circle around the word if it has a short **o** sound.

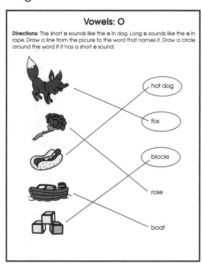

Page 165

Vowels: O

Directions: Say the name of each picture. If the picture has the long **o** sound, write a **green L** on the blank. If the picture has the short **o** sound, write a **red S** on the blank.

Page 166

Vowels: U

Directions: The short **u** sounds like the **u** in bug. The long **u** sounds like the **u** in blue. Draw a circle around the words with short **u**. Draw an **X** on the words with long **u**.

Page 167

Vowels: U

Directions: Say the name of each picture. If it has the long **u** sound, write a **u** in the **unicorn** column. If it has the short **u** sound, write a **u** in the **umbrella** column.

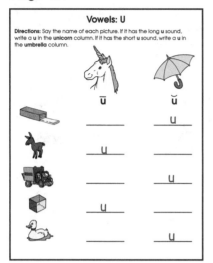

	ū	ŭ
	___	u
	u	___
	___	u
	u	___
	___	u

Page 168

Vowels: E

When you add an **e** to the end of some words, the vowel changes from a short vowel sound to a long vowel sound. The **e** is silent.

Example: rip + e = ripe

Directions: Say the word under the first picture in each pair. Then add an **e** to the word under the next picture. Say the new word.

pet — pete — tub — lube

man — mane — kit — kite

pin — pine — cap — cape

Page 169

Vowels

Directions: Say the name of each picture. Write the letter to complete each word.

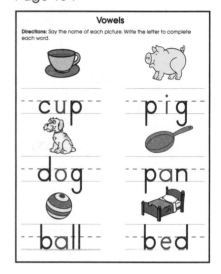

cup — pig

dog — pan

ball — bed

Page 170

Vowel Maze

Directions: Color your way through the maze by only coloring the vowels. Then write the five vowels below.

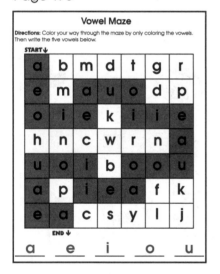

START ↓

a	b	m	d	t	g	r
e	m	a	u	o	d	p
o	i	e	k	i	i	e
h	n	c	w	r	n	a
u	o	i	b	o	o	a
a	p	i	e	a	f	k
e	a	c	s	y	l	j

END ↓

a e i o u

Page 171

Nouns

Directions: Draw a line to match each word with its picture.

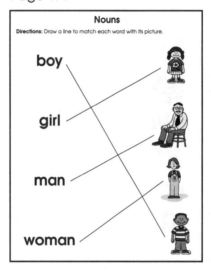

boy

girl

man

woman

Page 172

Nouns

Directions: Draw a line to match each word with its picture.

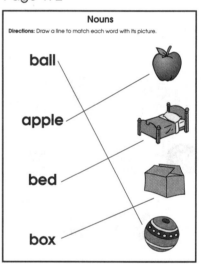

ball

apple

bed

box

Page 173

Nouns

Directions: Draw a line to match each word with its picture.

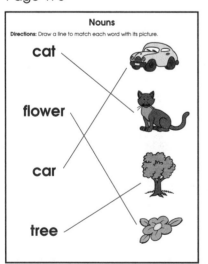

cat

flower

car

tree

Page 174

Verbs

Directions: Draw a line to match the action word with the person doing that action.

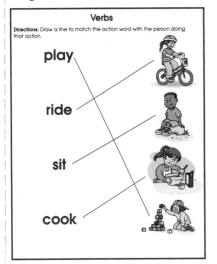

play

ride

sit

cook

Page 175

Nouns and Verbs

Directions: Cut out the words below. Glue naming words in the **Nouns** box. Glue action words in the **Verbs** box.

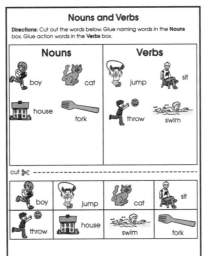

Nouns		Verbs	
boy	cat	jump	sit
house	fork	throw	swim

cut ✂ -

boy	jump	cat	sit
throw	house	swim	fork

Page 177

Verbs

Directions: Draw a line to match the action word with the person doing that action.

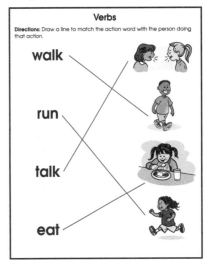

walk

run

talk

eat

Page 178

Animal Names

Directions: Fill in the missing letters for each word.

Example:

frog   frog

fish   fish

dog   dog

bird   bird

cat   cat

Page 179

Animal Names

Directions: The letters in the name of each animal are mixed up. Write each word correctly.

Example:

g f o r   frog

t a c   cat

o d g   dog

i f s h   fish

d i b r   bird

Page 180

Spelling

Directions: Write the word that completes each sentence. Put a **period** at the end of the telling sentences and a **question mark** at the end of the asking sentences.

Example: Does the sun shine on the flowers ?

| tree | grass | pond | sand | sky |

1. The sky was full of dark clouds⬚

2. Can you climb the tree ?

3. Did you see the duck in the pond ?

4. Is the child playing in the sand ?

5. The grass in the yard was tall⬚

Page 181

Spelling

Some words are opposites. Opposites are things that are different in every way. **Dark** and **light** are opposites.

Directions: Trace the letters to write each word. Then write the word again by yourself.

Example:

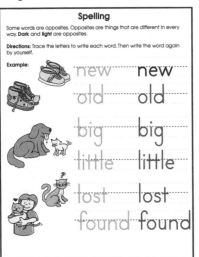

new   new

old   old

big   big

little little

lost   lost

found   found

Summer Link Super Edition Grade 1

Page 182

Sentences

Sentences begin with capital letters.

Directions: Read the sentences and write them below. Begin each sentence with a capital letter.

The cat is fat.

my dog is big.
My dog is big.

the boy is sad.
The boy is sad.

bikes are fun!
Bikes are fun!

dad can bake.
Dad can bake.

Page 183

Word Order Activity

Word order is the order of words in a sentence which makes sense.

Directions: Cut out the words and put them in the correct order. Glue each sentence on another sheet of paper.

I like to ride my bike

It is sunny and hot.

I can drink water.

My mom plays with me.

The dog can do tricks.

Can you go to the store?

Page 185

People Words

Sometimes we use other words in place of people names. For **boy** or **man**, we can use the word **he**. For **girl** or **woman**, we can use the word **she**. For two or more people, we can use the word **they**.

Directions: Write the words **he, she,** or **they** in these sentences.

Example: The boy likes cookies. He likes cookies.

1. The girl is running fast. She is running fast.

2. The man reads the paper. He reads the paper.

3. The woman has a cold. She has a cold.

4. Two children came to school. They came to school.

Page 186

Rhymes

Directions: Words that have the same ending sounds are called **rhyming** words. Circle the pairs that rhyme.

map   nest   dog   frog

hat   bat   kite   mop

can   fan   rat   pig

Page 187

Rhyming Pairs

Directions: Look at each pair of words and pictures. Circle the pairs that rhyme.

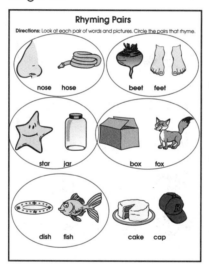

nose   hose   beet   feet

star   jar   box   fox

dish   fish   cake   cap

Page 188

Rhymes

Directions: Read the poem. Read the questions. Circle the correct answer.

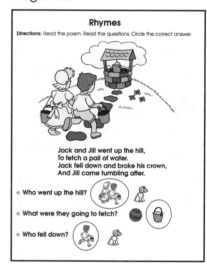

Jack and Jill went up the hill,
To fetch a pail of water.
Jack fell down and broke his crown,
And Jill came tumbling after.

◆ Who went up the hill?

◆ What were they going to fetch?

◆ Who fell down?

Page 189

Rhymes

Directions: Read about words that rhyme. Then circle the answers.

Words that rhyme have the same end sounds. **Wing** and **sing** rhyme. **Boy** and **toy** rhyme. **Dime** and **time** rhyme. Can you think of other words that rhyme?

1. Words that rhyme have the same (end letters / end sounds).

2. Time rhymes with (tree / dime).

TREE, SEE, SHOE, BLUE, KITE, BITE, MAKE, TAKE, FLY, BUY

Directions: Write one rhyme for each word.

wing   boy

Answers will vary.

dime   pink

Developmental Skills for First Grade Reading Success

This checklist is designed to help you assess your child's progress in the following kindergarten skills. You may want to add to or adapt this checklist to fit your child's abilities.

Basic Skills

- Names basic colors _____
- Names simple shapes _____
- Identifies opposites _____
- Understands positional concepts _____
- Names days of the week in order _____

Reading Readiness

- Follows multiple-step directions _____
- Recites the alphabet _____
- Identifies capital letters in random order _____
- Identifies lowercase letters in random order _____
- Matches capital and lowercase letters _____
- Identifies sounds made by letters _____
- Identifies characters in stories _____
- Identifies setting in stories _____
- Can retell a story _____
- Identifies problem/solution in a story _____
- Reads color words _____
- Reads some words by sight _____

Writing Readiness

- Dictates a sentence about a picture _____
- Writes from left to right _____
- Leaves spaces between words _____
- Writes some words independently _____
- Writes own sentences using sounds _____
- Uses punctuation in sentences _____

Fine (Small) Motor Skills

- Colors within lines _____
- Draws shapes _____
- Holds a pencil _____
- Prints letters and numbers _____
- Cuts a line with scissors _____

Reading Notes

Reading Notes

Reading Notes

Reading Notes

Reading Notes

Reading Notes

Reading Notes

This page intentionally left blank.

SUMMER LINK

SHAPES, NUMBERS, and LETTERS

This page intentionally left blank.

Name _____

Shapes

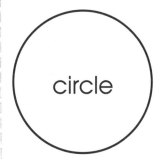 circle

□ square

▭ rectangle

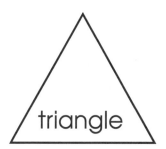 triangle

---

red	yellow	orange	purple
blue	green	black	brown

211   Summer Link Super Edition Grade 1

Numbers

Numbers

Uppercase Letters

Uppercase Letters

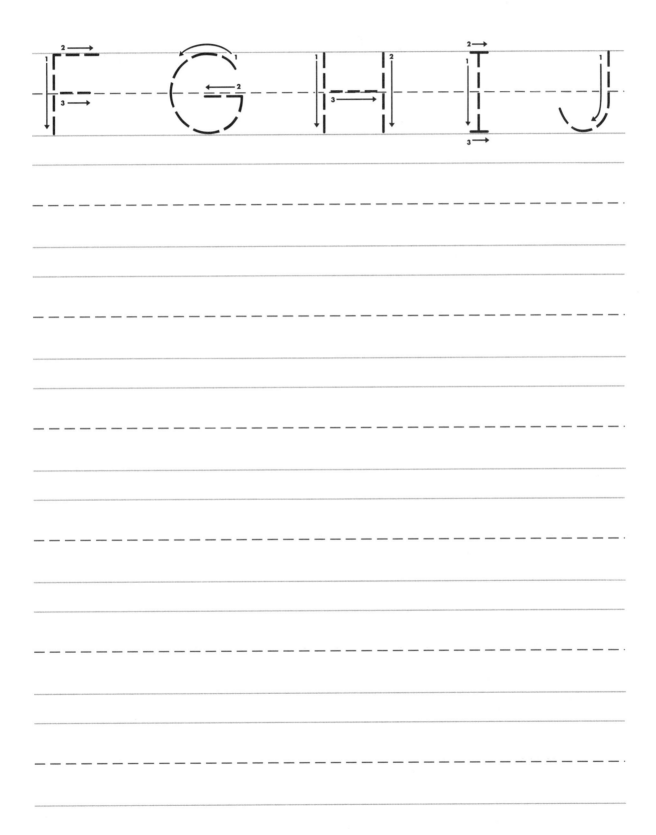

Name_____

Uppercase Letters

Uppercase Letters

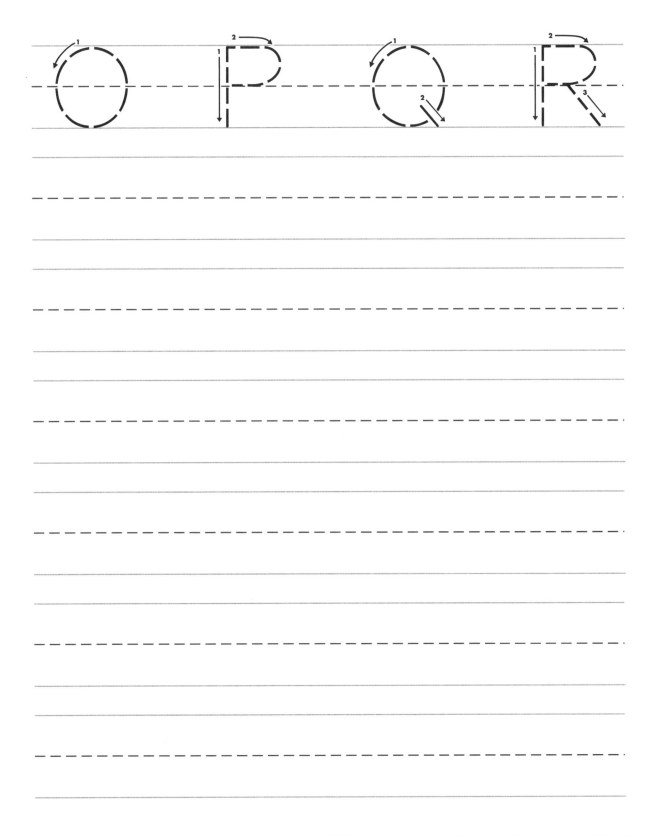

Uppercase Letters

Name _____

Uppercase Letters

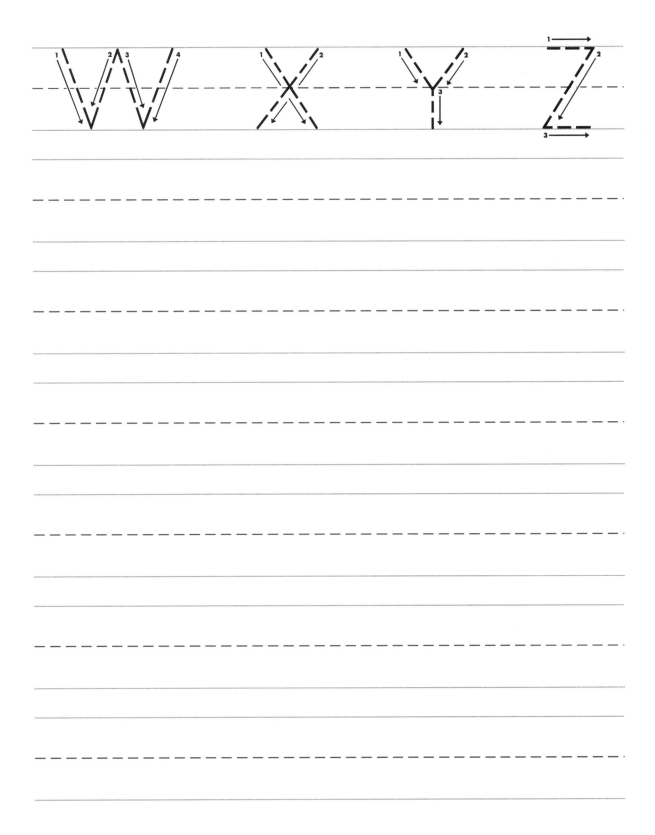

Lowercase Letters

Name _____

Lowercase Letters

Lowercase Letters

Lowercase Letters

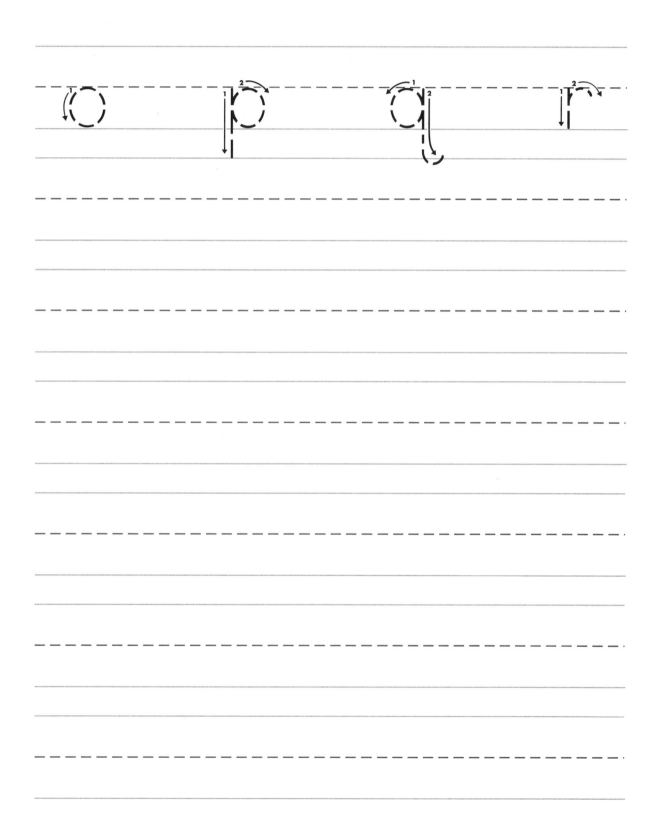

Name _____

Lowercase Letters

Lowercase Letters

w   x   y   z

This page intentionally left blank.

BASIC SKILLS

This page intentionally left blank.

Basic Skills

- Write your child's name on a sheet of paper. Then have your child trace over it with different colored markers to make a rainbow effect.

- Create "name art" with your child. Have your child write his/her name on a sheet of paper and illustrate it.

- Help your child learn his/her full name, address and telephone number. Explain situations when it is important for your child to be able to provide this information.

- Sing and dance the "Hokey Pokey" with your child to practice the concepts of left and right.

- Discuss types of weather. Ask your child to identify the clothes that he/she would wear when the weather is rainy, snowy, hot, etc.

- Look at family pictures with your child. Discuss some of the things that are the same about family members as well as some of the things that make them unique individuals.

- Talk with your child about foods he/she likes to eat. Talk about why they are good for you and where they come from. Help your child understand where foods come from before they go to the grocery store. Group foods by food group: fruits, vegetables, sweets, grains, etc.

- Find pictures of animals and have your child name them. Help your child learn the names for the animal babies and the sounds the animals make.

- Talk about the importance of trees to our environment (homes for animals, food, shade, clean air). You may want to read the book A Tree Is Nice by Janet May Udry.

- Plant seeds with your child and keep a record of what happens. Talk about the order in which the changes occur.

- Make a chart with your child that lists his/her daily routine. For example: 8 o'clock—time to get up. Talk about the sequence in which he/she does things.

- Have a "Things That Go Together" scavenger hunt. Make a list of things found around the house that need "partners" (or use the objects themselves) and have your child search the house for them. For example: A toothbrush needs _____. Peanut butter needs _____.

- Play a color search game. Ask your child to find as many things as he/she can that are the color you name.

- Buy fingerpaints and allow your child to experiment, mixing them to make other colors.

- Bake a cake or make cutout cookies with your child and allow him/her to mix food coloring into white frosting to create different colors of frosting.

- Set out an assortment of dried beans. Have your child sort them into piles by shape, size, and color.

- Take a walk with your child and encourage him/her to pick up "treasures" along the way. After returning home, ask your child how he/she could sort the treasures into groups and have him/her do so.

- Have your child put away the silverware. Have him/her sort the forks, knives, small spoons and large spoons.

- Have your child organize his/her clothes by type or color.

- Talk with your child about ways his/her toys and books could be organized by how they are alike in color, size, etc.

- Play "Mommy or Daddy Says" the same way "Simon Says" is played. Give your child verbal directions. He/she is only to follow them if preceded by the words "Mommy Says" or "Daddy Says."

- Give your child directions in three or four steps. Say them clearly and in order, holding up a finger as you say each one. See how well your child can remember your directions and follow them.

- Look for shapes around the house. Make a list of things that are circles, squares, rectangles, and triangles.

Squares	Circles

- Make a geoboard for your child. Pound equally spaced rows of nails into a square piece of wood. Using rubber bands, have your child create different shapes on the geoboard.

- Help your child observe shapes in nature. Take a walk and collect leaves, seeds, nuts, stones, etc. Have your child sort them into groups by shape, then by color and size.

- Find opportunities around the house to compare things that are big and small. Have your child compare objects, focusing on their size.

- Have your child trace your hand. Then have your child trace his/her own hand and compare the sizes. Whose hand is bigger? Whose is smaller? Who has longer fingers? Whose fingers are shorter?

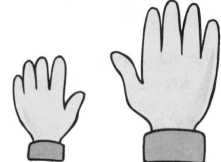

- Have your child use paper clips to measure things around the house. Challenge him/her to think of other units that could be used to measure (spoons, pencils, etc.).

- Take out different-sized glasses and cups. Let your child experiment filling and emptying them. Talk to your child about the concepts of full and empty.

- While experimenting with the cups, help your child count the number of times you must pour liquid from a small cup to fill a larger one. Talk about the relationship between sizes.

- Have your child make a bead necklace using a pattern that he/she develops. Check to be sure there is consistency throughout the pattern.

- Lay similar objects on the table in a pattern and have your child identify the pattern.

• Set objects on, below and between each other on the kitchen table. Ask your child where the objects are located. Have your child move the objects and quiz you!

Reading

• Read to and with your child every day to foster a lifelong love of books and reading. Let your child sit on your lap or beside you so that he/she can see the pictures as you read. Point to the words you read, and if there are repeated refrains in the books you read, pause at those points and let your child supply the words.

• Be sure your child sees you reading. Let him/her know how important reading is in your life, both at home and on the job.

• Call attention to the pictures in the books you read and talk about them with your child.

• Stop as you are reading a story and ask your child what he/she thinks will happen next.

• Talk to your child about the characters in the stories and the setting.

• Talk about the sequence of the story. Have your child tell you what happened first, in the middle, and at the end.

- Help your child understand that print has meaning by encouraging him/her to "read" cereal boxes and other print around the house.

- Look for print on street and business signs and have your child "read" it. Explain what these signs mean and why they are important.

- Encourage your child to point out letters he/she recognizes in print and practice spelling words he/she sees frequently. Use magazines, newspapers and coloring books to help your child create letter and word collages.

- Label objects around the house so that your child will learn to associate the object with the printed word. Index cards written with colored markers work well.

- Focus on a "letter of the day" (or week) in your home. Help your child look for that letter in print and think of words that begin with that letter.

- Create a chart labeled with color words. Go through magazines with your child and let him/her find pictures that are that color, gluing them on the correct section of the chart.

- Go through the grocery ads and have your child cut out the pictures and words. Play a matching game.

- Buy magnetic letters and put them on the refrigerator. Encourage your child to spell words with them.

- Create your own ABC book or list of words your child can write. Let your child illustrate the book.

- Play "I Spy" with your child. ("I spy something that begins with the letter A.") Have your child guess what it is.

- Play "I'm Thinking of a Letter." Give your child different clues about a letter. See how many clues it takes for him/her to guess it. Then have your child think of a letter for you to guess.

- Have your child shape cooked spaghetti into each of the letters of the alphabet. He/she could then make objects that begin with each letter.

- Give your child old magazines. Give him/her directions such as "Circle all the m's." Continue with various directions, making sure to include different letters of the alphabet.

- Make sugar cookie dough and have your child form letters and words with the dough. Then bake the letters and let your child eat his/her favorite words. Don't forget to have him/her say the sound the letter makes as he/she eats it.

- Go through photo albums and let your child select a picture from each year of his/her life. Help your child sequence them. He/she may want to write his/her age or a brief caption underneath each picture.

- Encourage relatives or friends to send postcards or special occasion cards to your child to encourage him/her to read.

- Make frequent trips to the library and let your child explore the books there, choosing some favorites to take home for you to read.

- Ask grandparents, other family members or friends to recommend books that they liked as a child and have them tell your child why they liked them.

- Arrange a book swap with families of other young children so the children can read their friends' favorite books.

- Have your child dictate a story using greeting card or magazine pictures. Write the story for your child and help him/her read it.

Writing

- Provide your child with many different writing materials—pens, pencils, markers, crayons, paints—and many kinds of paper—writing paper, greeting cards, postcards, invitations, etc. Encourage your child to write and to draw illustrations.

- Keep your child's writing materials in a special place where they can be used independently.

- Buy a notebook for your child's writing. Let him/her decorate it and make it special. Encourage your child to write in the notebook every day. When your child writes something, provide opportunities for him/her to share it with you.

- When your child draws a picture, have him/her write a caption or dictate a caption for you to write. Be sure to write exactly what your child dictates.

- Encourage your child to help you when you are writing: making grocery lists, writing notes and letters, etc. Talk about how writing is important to you.

- Provide chalk and a chalkboard for your child.

- Spend time writing outdoors with your child. Write with sidewalk chalk all over the driveway.

- Take a trip to the beach with your child and use sticks to write words in the sand. Read what you write to each other.

- Enter art/coloring/writing contests often. This encourages creativity, finished work, and the idea of publishing your child's work.

- Use your computer as a writing tool. Have your child type the alphabet or short messages on the screen. Print out the finished product.

- Make pudding with your child. Spread it on a cookie sheet and let your child write words he/she knows with his/her fingers!

- When on a trip, help your child write postcards home to family and friends.

- Write a book about your child and your family. Use pictures of family members or events. Have your child dictate captions to you or let him/her write them him/herself. Punch holes in the pages and fasten them together.

Math

- Encourage your child to find numbers around the house (clocks, television, telephone, etc.) and tell you how they are used.

- Look for and read numbers as you ride in the car: street signs, house numbers, at gas stations and other businesses, license plate numbers, etc.

- Tell your child how you use numbers in your job and at home.

- Look for numbers in the grocery store. Have your child help you find the prices of items.

- Label different household items with "prices" and play store with your child.

- Capitalize on everyday opportunities to count with your child and to have him/her practice counting. Count cans in the cupboard as you put them away, count books on the bookshelf or toys as they are picked up.

- Have your child listen and identify the number of times that you make a special noise like clapping or snapping your fingers.

- Let your child play counting and number games with blocks. For example, count how many blocks tall you can make a tower before it topples!

- Make number cards from index cards. Write a number from 1 to 20 on each card and have your child practice putting them in order.

- Give your child a number card and a supply of small objects (macaroni, beads, blocks, etc.) and have him/her practice counting the correct number of objects. Let your child practice with many different numbers. Then count out a number of objects and have your child match the correct number card to it.

- Say a number and have your child tell you what number comes after it or before it.

- Use magazine pictures to make a counting book. Write a number on each page and have your child cut out pictures of that number of objects on the page.

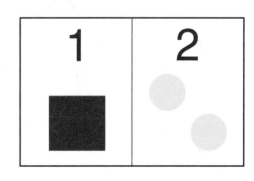

- Find numbers in catalogs and let your child practice reading them.

- Punch ten holes in an old greeting card cover with a nice picture. Number the holes. Give your child a piece of string and have him/her thread the holes in the correct order.

- Sing "This Old Man" with your child, having him/her use fingers to represent the numbers.

- Look for books and songs that incorporate numbers, such as Ten Sly Piranhas by William Wise.

- Use the calendar to help your child with number recognition. Talk with your child about the date and month and count the number of days until a special event.

- Place different numbers of objects in an egg carton to give your child practice counting numbers to 12.

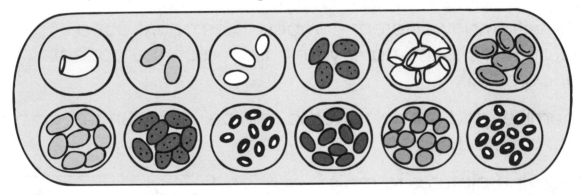

- Number clothespins from 1 to 12. Label index cards with the number words on one side and the corresponding number of dots on the other side. Play a game with your child, having him/her clip the clothespins on the correct card.

- Challenge your child to count back from 10.

- Have your child practice counting by tens. Hold up all ten fingers each time he/she says a number.

- Have your child shape clay into each of the numbers from 1 to 20.

- Draw a number on your child's back with your finger. Have your child tell you what number you drew. Then let your child draw a number on your back.

- Read The M&M's Counting Book by Barbara Barbieri McGrath with your child. Then do some of the suggested activities.

- Talk with your child about ways he/she helps at home. Ask: How can learning to count help us in setting the table?

- Put out a small pile of coins and have your child practice sorting and naming them. Have pennies, nickels, dimes, and quarters available for your child to manipulate. Have your child count how many there are of each coin and talk about the value of each coin.

- Have your child help set the table. Help him/her use one napkin for each plate, one fork for each napkin, etc.

• Using a bag of marshmallows, have your child give you some marshmallows and take some for him/herself. Talk about who has more and who has fewer. Then, divide the marshmallows equally.

TEST PRACTICE

About the Tests

What Are Standardized Achievement Tests?

Achievement tests measure what children know in particular subject areas such as reading, language arts, and mathematics. They do not measure your child's intelligence or ability to learn.

When tests are standardized, or *normed*, children's test results are compared with those of a specific group who have taken the test, usually at the same age or grade.

Standardized achievement tests measure what children around the country are learning. The test makers survey popular textbook series, as well as state curriculum frameworks and other professional sources, to determine what content is covered widely.

Because of variations in state frameworks and text-book series, as well as grade ranges on some test levels, the tests may cover some material that children have not yet learned. This is especially true if the test is offered early in the school year. However, test scores are compared to those of other children who take the test at the same time of year, so your child will not be at a disadvantage if his or her class has not covered specific material yet.

Different School Districts, Different Tests

There are many flexible options for districts when offering standardized tests. Many school districts choose not to give the full test battery, but select certain content and scoring options. For example, many schools may test only in the areas of reading and mathematics. Similarly, a state or district may use one test for certain grades and another test for other grades. These decisions are often based on the amount of time and money a district wishes to spend on test administration. Some states choose to develop their own statewide assessment tests.

On pages 245 and 246 you will find information about these five widely used standardized achievement tests:

- California Achievement Test (CAT)
- Terra Nova/CTBS
- Iowa Test of Basic Skills (ITBS)
- Stanford Achievement Test (SAT9)
- Metropolitan Achievement Test (MAT)

However, this book contains strategies and practice questions for use with a variety of tests. Even if your state does not give one of the five tests listed above, your child will benefit from doing the practice questions in this book. If you're unsure about which test your child takes, contact your local school district to find out which tests are given.

Types of Test Questions

Traditionally, standardized achievement tests have used only multiple-choice questions. Today, many tests may include constructed response (short answer) and extended response (essay) questions as well.

In addition, many tests include questions that tap students' higher-order thinking skills. Instead of simple recall questions, such as identifying a date in history, questions may require students to make comparisons and contrasts or analyze results, among other skills.

What the Tests Measure

These tests do not measure your child's level of intelligence, but they do show how well your child knows material that he or she has learned and that is

also covered on the tests. It's important to remember that some tests cover content that is not taught in your child's school or grade. In other instances, depending on when in the year the test is given, your child may not yet have covered the material.

If the test reports you receive show that your child needs improvement in one or more skill areas, you may want to seek help from your child's teacher and find out how you can work with your child to improve his or her skills.

California Achievement Test (CAT/5)

What Is the California Achievement Test?

The *California Achievement Test* is a standardized achievement test battery that is widely used with elementary through high school students.

Parts of the Test

The *CAT* includes tests in the following content areas:

Reading
- Word Analysis
- Vocabulary
- Comprehension

Spelling

Language Arts
- Language Mechanics
- Language Usage

Mathematics

Science

Social Studies

Your child may take some or all of these subtests if your district uses the *California Achievement Test*.

Terra Nova/CTBS (Comprehensive Tests of Basic Skills)

What Is the Terra Nova/CTBS?

The *Terra Nova/Comprehensive Tests of Basic Skills* is a standardized achievement test battery used in elementary through high school grades.

While many of the test questions on the *Terra Nova* are in the traditional multiple choice form, your child may take parts of the *Terra Nova* that include some open-ended questions (constructed-response items).

Parts of the Test

Your child may take some or all of the following subtests if your district uses the *Terra Nova/CTBS*:

Reading/Language Arts

Mathematics

Science

Social Studies

Supplementary tests include:
- Word Analysis
- Vocabulary
- Language Mechanics
- Spelling
- Mathematics Computation

Critical thinking skills may also be tested.

Iowa Test of Basic Skills (ITBS)

What Is the ITBS?

The *Iowa Test of Basic Skills* is a standardized achievement test battery used in elementary through high school grades.

Parts of the Test

Your child may take some or all of these subtests if your district uses the *ITBS*, also known as the *Iowa*:

Reading
- Vocabulary
- Reading Comprehension

Language Arts
- Spelling
- Capitalization
- Punctuation
- Usage and Expression

Math
- Concepts/Estimate
- Problems/Data Interpretation

Social Studies

Science

Sources of Information

Stanford Achievement Test (SAT9)

What Is the Stanford Achievement Test?

The *Stanford Achievement Test, Ninth Edition (SAT9)* is a standardized achievement test battery used in elementary through high school grades.

Note that the *Stanford Achievement Test (SAT9)* is a different test from the *SAT* used by high school students for college admissions.

While many of the test questions on the *SAT9* are in traditional multiple choice form, your child may take parts of *the SAT9* that include some open-ended questions (constructed-response items).

Parts of the Test

Your child may take some or all of these subtests if your district uses the *Stanford Achievement Test*:

Reading
- Vocabulary
- Reading Comprehension

Mathematics
- Problem Solving
- Procedures

Language Arts

Spelling

Study Skills

Listening
Critical thinking skills may also be tested.

Metropolitan Achievement Test (MAT7 and MAT8)

What Is the Metropolitan Achievement Test?

The *Metropolitan Achievement Test* is a standardized achievement test battery used in elementary through high school grades.

Parts of the Test

Your child may take some or all of these subtests if your district uses the *Metropolitan Achievement Test*:

Reading
- Vocabulary
- Reading Comprehension

Math
- Concepts and Problem Solving
- Computation

Language Arts
- Pre-writing
- Composing
- Editing

Science

Social Studies

Research Skills

Thinking Skills

Spelling

Statewide Assessments

Today the majority of states give statewide assessments. In some cases these tests are known as *high-stakes assessments*. This means that students must score at a certain level in order to be promoted. Some states use minimum competency or proficiency tests. Often these tests measure more basic skills than other types of statewide assessments.

Statewide assessments are generally linked to state curriculum frameworks. Frameworks provide a blueprint, or outline, to ensure that teachers are covering the same curriculum topics as other teachers in the same grade level in the state. In some states, standardized achievement tests (such as the five described in this book) are used in connection with statewide assessments.

When Statewide Assessments Are Given

Statewide assessments may not be given at every grade level. Generally, they are offered at one or more grades in elementary school, middle school, and high school. Many states test at grades 4, 8, and 10.

State-by-State Information

You can find information about statewide assessments and curriculum frameworks at your state Department of Education Web site. To find the address for your individual state, go to www.ed.gov, click on Topics A–Z, and then click on State Departments of Education. You will find a list of all the state departments of education, mailing addresses, and Web sites.

How to Help Your Child Prepare for Standardized Testing

Preparing All Year Round

Perhaps the most valuable way you can help your child prepare for standardized achievement tests is by providing enriching experiences. Keep in mind also that test results for younger children are not as reliable as for older students. If a child is hungry, tired, or upset, this may result in a poor test score. Here are some tips on how you can help your child do his or her best on standardized tests.

Read aloud with your child. Reading aloud helps develop vocabulary and fosters a positive attitude toward reading. Reading together is one of the most effective ways you can help your child succeed in school.

Share experiences. Baking cookies together, planting a garden, or making a map of your neighborhood are examples of activities that help build skills that are measured on the tests, such as sequencing and following directions.

Become informed about your state's testing procedures. Ask about or watch for announcements of meetings that explain about standardized tests and statewide assessments in your school district. Talk to your child's teacher about your child's individual performance on these state tests during a parent-teacher conference.

Help your child know what to expect. Read and discuss with your child the test-taking tips in this book. Your child can prepare by working through a couple of strategies a day so that no practice session takes too long.

Help your child with his or her regular school assignments. Set up a quiet study area for homework. Supply this area with pencils, paper, markers, a calculator, a ruler, a dictionary, scissors, glue, and so on. Check your child's homework and offer to help if he or she gets stuck. But remember, it's your child's homework, not yours. If you help too much, your child will not benefit from the activity.

Keep in regular contact with your child's teacher. Attend parent-teacher conferences, school functions, PTA or PTO meetings, and school board meetings. This will help you get to know the educators in your district and the families of your child's classmates.

Learn to use computers as an educational resource. If you do not have a computer and Internet access at home, try your local library.

Remember—simply getting your child comfortable with testing procedures and helping him or her know what to expect can improve test scores!

Getting Ready for the Big Day

There are lots of things you can do on or immediately before test day to improve your child's chances of testing success. What's more, these strategies will help your child prepare him-or herself for school tests, too, and promote general study skills that can last a lifetime.

Provide a good breakfast on test day. Instead of sugar cereal, which provides immediate but not long-term energy, have your child eat a breakfast with protein or complex carbohydrates, such as an egg, whole grain cereal or toast, or a banana-yogurt shake.

Assure your child that he or she is not expected to know all of the answers on the test. Explain that other children in higher grades may take the same test, and that the test may measure things your child has not yet learned in school. Help your child understand that you expect him or her to put forth a good effort—and that this is enough. Your child should not try to cram for these tests. Also avoid threats or bribes; these put undue pressure on children and may interfere with their best performance.

Promote a good night's sleep. A good night's sleep before the test is essential. Try not to overstress the importance of the test. This may cause your child to lose sleep because of anxiety. Doing some exercise after school and having a quiet evening routine will help your child sleep well the night before the test.

Keep the mood light and offer encouragement. To provide a break on test days, do something fun and special after school—take a walk around the neighborhood, play a game, read a favorite book, or prepare a special snack together. These activities keep your child's mood light—even if the testing sessions have been difficult—and show how much you appreciate your child's effort.

Taking Standardized Tests

What You Need to Know About Taking Tests

You can get better at taking tests. Here are some tips.

Do your schoolwork.

Study in school. Do your homework all the time. These things will help you in school and on any tests you take. Learn new things a little at a time. Then you will remember them better when you see them on a test.

Feel your best.

One way you can do your best on tests and in school is to make sure your body is ready. Get a good night's sleep. Eat a healthy breakfast.

One more thing: Wear comfortable clothes. You can also wear your lucky shirt or your favorite color on test day. It can't hurt. It may even make you feel better about the test.

Be ready for the test.

Do practice questions. Learn about the different kinds of questions. Books like this one will help you.

Follow the test directions.

Listen carefully to the directions your teacher gives. Read all instructions carefully. Watch out for words such as *not*, *none*, *never*, *all*, and *always*. These words can change the meaning of the directions. You may want to circle words like these. This will help you keep them in mind as you answer the questions.

Look carefully at each page before you start.

Do reading tests in a special order. First, read the directions. Read the questions next. This way you will know what to look for as you read. Then read the story. Last, read the story again quickly. Skim it to find the best answer.

On math tests, look at the labels on graphs and charts.

Think about what the graph or chart shows. You will often need to draw conclusions about the information to answer some questions.

Use your time wisely. Many tests have time limits. Look at the clock when the test starts. Figure out when you need to stop. When you begin, look over the whole thing. Do the easy parts first. Go back and do the hard parts last. Make sure you do not spend too much time on any one part. This way, if you run out of time, you still have completed much of the test.

Fill in the answer circles the right way. Fill in the whole circle. Make your pencil mark dark, but not so dark that it goes through the paper! Be sure you pick just one answer for each question. If you pick two answers, both will be marked as wrong.

Use context clues to figure out hard questions. You may come across a word or an idea you don't under-stand. First, try to say it in your own words. Then use context clues—the words in the sentences nearby— to help you figure out its meaning.

Sometimes it's good to guess. Here's what to do. Each question may have four or five answer choices. You may know that two answers are wrong, but you are not sure about the rest. Then make your best guess. If you are not sure about any of the answers, skip it. Do not guess. Tests like these take away extra points for wrong answers. So it is better to leave them blank.

Check your work. You may finish the test before the time is up. Then you can go back and check your answers. Make sure you answered each question you could. Also, make sure that you filled in only one answer circle for each question. Erase any extra marks on the page.

Finally—stay calm! Take time to relax before the test. One good way to relax is to get some exercise. Stretch, shake out your fingers, and wiggle your toes. Take a few slow, deep breaths. Then picture yourself doing a great job!

Getting Ready All Year

You can do better in school and on tests if you know how to study and make good use of your time. Here are some tips.

Make it easy to get your homework done. Set up a place in which to do it each day. Choose a place that is quiet. Get the things you need, such as pencils, paper, and markers. Put them in your homework place.

Homework Log and Weekly Calendar Make your own homework log. Or copy the one on pages 254–255 of this book. Write down your homework each day. Also list other things you have to do, such as sports practice or music lessons. Then you won't forget easily.

Do your homework right away. Do it soon after you get home from school. Give yourself a lot of time. Then you won't be too tired to do it later on.

Get help if you need it. If you need help, just ask. Call a friend. Or ask a family member. If they cannot help you, ask your teacher the next day.

Figure out how you learn best. Some people learn best by listening, others by looking. Some learn best by doing something with their hands or moving around. Some children like to work in groups. And some are very happy working alone.

Think about your favorite parts of school. Are you good in art, mathematics, or maybe gym? Your favorite class maybe a clue to how you learn best. Try to figure it out. Then use it to study and learn better.

Practice, practice, practice! The best way to get better is by practicing a lot. You may have trouble in a school subject. Do some extra work in that subject. It can give you just the boost you need.

	MONDAY	TUESDAY	WEDNESDAY
MATHEMATICS			
READING			
LANGUAGE ARTS			
OTHER			

THURSDAY	FRIDAY	SATURDAY/SUNDAY	
$\begin{array}{r} 2 \\ +3 \\ \hline 5 \end{array}$			MATHEMATICS
			READING
			LANGUAGE ARTS
			OTHER

The following Test Practice pages are designed to help your child become familiar with the format of standardized tests using content that they understand.

First, read the instructions on each Test Practice page aloud to your child. Then, explain to your child that in this section, he or she will choose his or her answers by filling in small circular answer "bubbles."

Walk your child through each page, and offer him or her assistance with difficulties. When your kindergartner is presented with his or her first standardized test, he or she will have the added benefit of being familiar with the format.

Name _____

Directions: Fill in the answer bubble under the circle in each row.

 Tip: Remember to fill in the answer bubble completely.

     O   O   O

     O   O   O

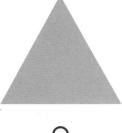  

     O   O   O

Summer Link Super Edition Grade 1

Name _____

Directions: Fill in the answer bubble under the square in each row.

**Tip:** Remember to fill in the answer bubble completely.

○   ○   ○

○   ○   ○

○   ○   ○

Name _____

Directions: Fill in the answer bubble under the triangle in each row.

 Tip: Remember to fill in the answer bubble completely.

○   ○   ○

○   ○   ○

○   ○   ○

Name _____

Directions: Fill in the answer bubble under the rectangle in each row.

 **Tip:** Remember to fill in the answer bubble completely.

○   ○   ○

○   ○   ○

○   ○   ○

Tip: Remember to fill in the answer bubble completely.

Directions: Fill in the answer bubble under the circle.

○   ○   ○

Fill in the answer bubble under the square.

○   ○   ○

Fill in the answer bubble under the triangle.

○   ○   ○

Name _____

Directions: Fill in the answer bubble under the oval in each row.

 **Tip:** Remember to fill in the answer bubble completely.

      (oval)

○   ○   ○

○   ○   ○

○   ○   ○

Name _____

Directions: Fill in the answer bubble under the diamond in each row.

 Tip: Remember to fill in the answer bubble completely.

○   ○   ○

_____

○   ○   ○

_____

○   ○   ○

Directions: Fill in the answer bubble under the star in each row.

 **Tip:** Remember to fill in the answer bubble completely.

○   ○   ○

○   ○   ○

○   ○   ○

Name _____

Directions: Fill in the answer bubble under the heart in each row.

 Tip: Remember to fill in the answer bubble completely.

○   ○   ○

○   ○   ○

○   ○   ○

Name _____

Directions: Fill in the answer bubble under the shape in each row that is different.

Tip: Remember to fill in the answer bubble completely.

 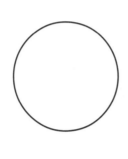 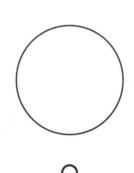 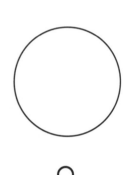

○　　　　○　　　　○　　　　○

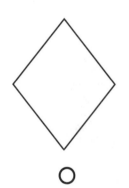 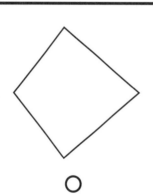 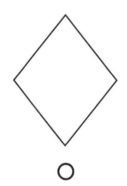 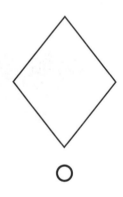

○　　　　○　　　　○　　　　○

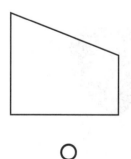 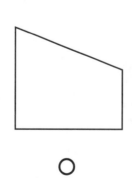  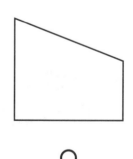

○　　　　○　　　　○　　　　○

Name _____

Directions: Find the shape in each row that looks the same as the first shape. Fill in its answer bubble.

Tip: Remember to fill in the answer bubble completely.

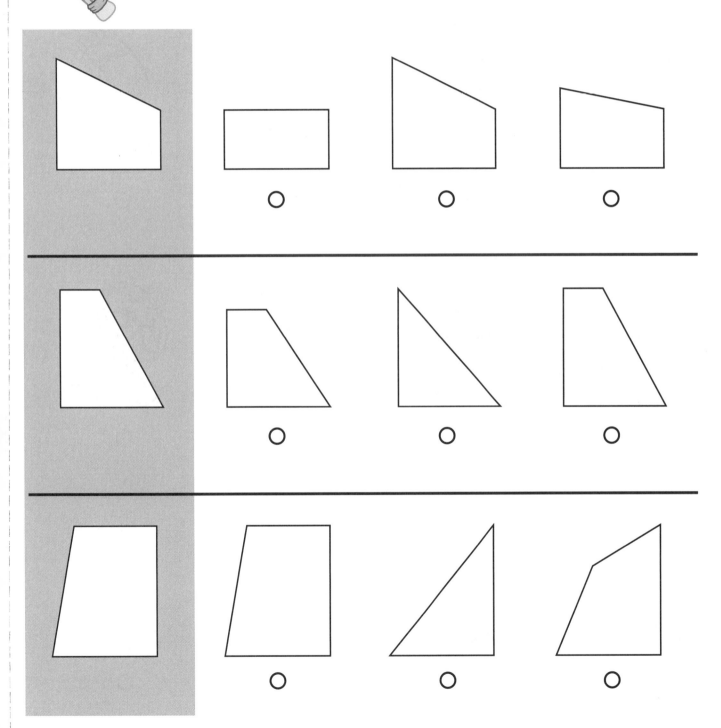

Directions: Find the picture in each row that does not belong. Fill in its answer bubble.

Tip: Remember to fill in the answer bubble completely.

Name _____

Directions: Find the picture in each row that does not belong. Fill in its answer bubble.

Tip: Remember to fill in the answer bubble completely.

   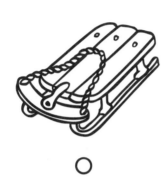      

○   ○   ○   ○

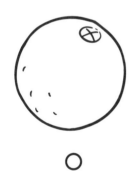         

○   ○   ○   ○

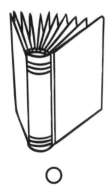      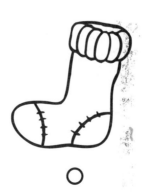   

○   ○   ○   ○

Tip: Remember to fill in the answer bubble completely.

Directions: Fill in the answer bubble under the picture that is small.

O   O

Fill in the answer bubble under the picture that is big.

O   O

Tip: Remember to fill in the answer bubble completely.

Directions: Find the picture that is above the cloud. Fill in its answer bubble.

Find the picture that is below the cloud. Fill in its answer bubble.

○

○

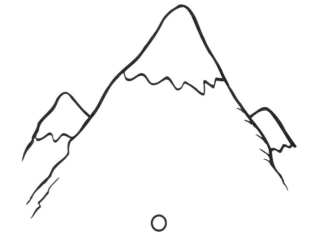

○

○

271

Directions: Find the shape that is between the other shapes. Fill in its answer bubble.

Tip: Remember to fill in the answer bubble completely.

⬚   ⬚   ⬚

○   ○   ○

Tip: Remember to fill in the answer bubble completely.

Directions: Fill in the answer bubble under the picture on the left.

○   ○

Fill in the answer bubble under the picture on the right.

○   ○

Directions: Fill in the answer bubble under the letter that matches the first letter in each row.

Tip: Remember to fill in the answer bubble completely.

A	N	V	A
	○	○	○
a	b	c	a
	○	○	○
B	B	C	A
	○	○	○
b	d	a	b
	○	○	○
C	O	D	C
	○	○	○
c	a	c	o
	○	○	○

Name _____

Directions: Fill in the answer bubble under the letter that matches the first letter in each row.

Tip: Remember to fill in the answer bubble completely.

D	B ○	G ○	D ○
d	b ○	d ○	a ○
E	H ○	F ○	E ○
e	e ○	a ○	b ○
F	E ○	F ○	A ○
f	t ○	f ○	l ○

275   **Summer Link Super Edition Grade 1**

Name _____

Directions: Fill in the answer bubble under the letter that matches the first letter in each row.

Tip: Remember to fill in the answer bubble completely.

G	C ○	G ○	O ○
g	g ○	p ○	q ○
H	E ○	F ○	H ○
h	n ○	b ○	h ○
I	H ○	I ○	L ○
i	t ○	i ○	l ○

Directions: Fill in the answer bubble under the letter that matches the first letter in each row.

Tip: Remember to fill in the answer bubble completely.

J	J	U	L
	○	○	○
j	g	j	i
	○	○	○
K	N	H	K
	○	○	○
k	h	k	b
	○	○	○
L	J	I	L
	○	○	○
l	t	i	l
	○	○	○

Directions: Fill in the answer bubble under the letter that matches the first letter in each row.

Tip: Remember to fill in the answer bubble completely.

M	H ○	M ○	L ○
m	M ○	m ○	n ○
N	M ○	N ○	m ○
n	n ○	m ○	a ○
O	O ○	D ○	B ○
o	a ○	O ○	o ○

Directions: Fill in the answer bubble under the letter that matches the first letter in each row.

Tip: Remember to fill in the answer bubble completely.

P	D ○	P ○	b ○
p	p ○	d ○	b ○
Q	O ○	G ○	Q ○
q	p ○	q ○	d ○
R	B ○	P ○	R ○
r	n ○	m ○	r ○

Directions: Fill in the answer bubble under the letter that matches the first letter in each row.

Tip: Remember to fill in the answer bubble completely.

S	P ○	S ○	B ○
s	a ○	s ○	e ○
T	I ○	L ○	T ○
t	f ○	t ○	i ○
U	D ○	U ○	O ○
u	u ○	n ○	m ○

Name _____

Directions: Fill in the answer bubble under the letter that matches the first letter in each row.

Tip: Remember to fill in the answer bubble completely.

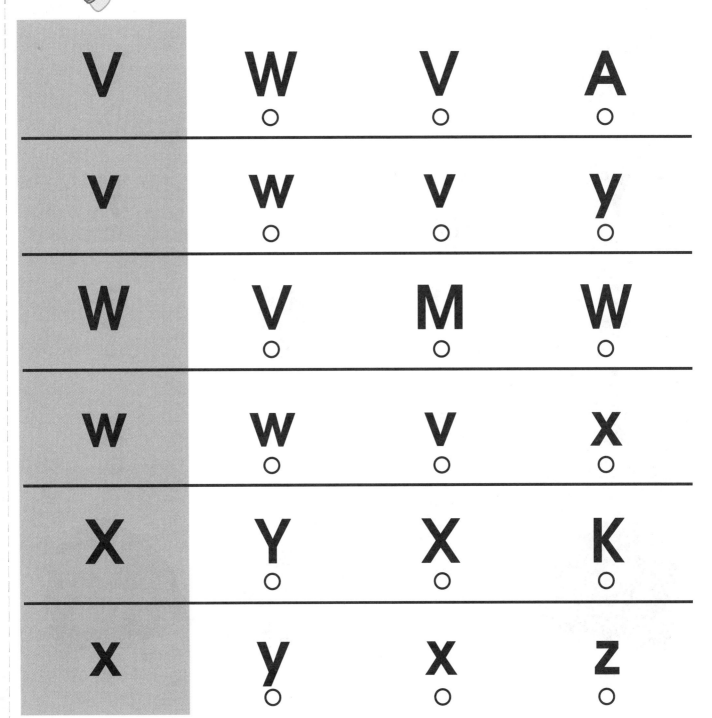

V	W ○	V ○	A ○
V	W ○	V ○	y ○
W	V ○	M ○	W ○
W	W ○	V ○	X ○
X	Y ○	X ○	K ○
X	y ○	X ○	Z ○

281   **Summer Link Super Edition Grade 1**

Name _____

Directions: Fill in the answer bubble under the letter that matches the first letter in each row.

 **Tip:** Remember to fill in the answer bubble completely.

Y	W ○	Y ○	V ○
y	W ○	V ○	y ○
Z	N ○	M ○	Z ○
z	n ○	z ○	x ○

Name _____

Directions: Fill in the answer bubble under each fish that has an uppercase and lowercase letter that match.

 **Tip:** Remember to fill in the answer bubble completely.

Oo

○

Oc

○

Nm

○

Nn

○

Nz

○

Mm

○

Summer Link Super Edition Grade 1

Directions: Find the picture in each row that begins with the letter shown. Fill in its answer bubble.

Tip: Remember to fill in the answer bubble completely.

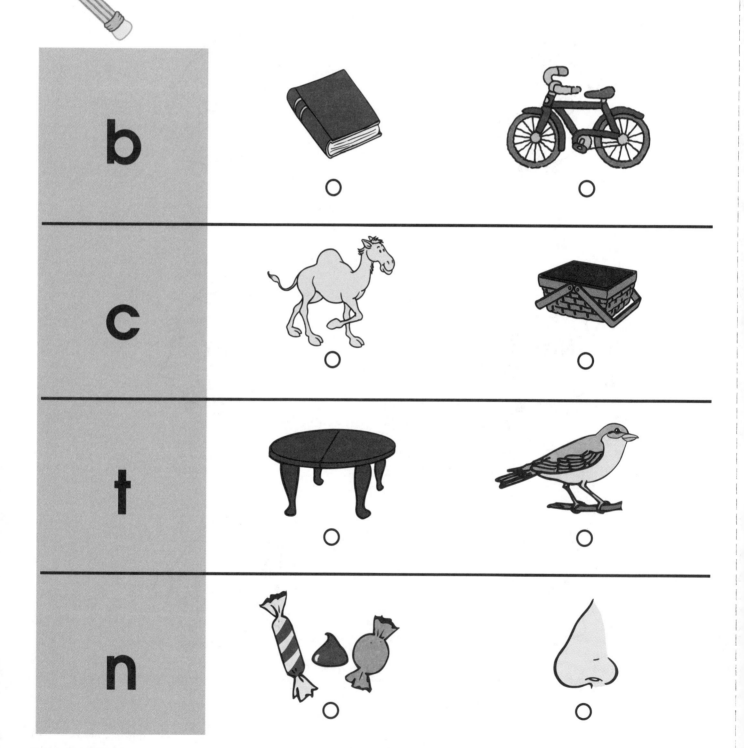

b

○   ○

c

○   ○

t

○   ○

n

○   ○

Name _____

Directions: Find the picture in each row that has the same beginning sound as the colored picture. Fill in its answer bubble.

Tip: Remember to fill in the answer bubble completely.

○

○

○

○

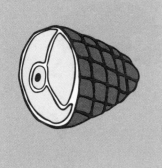

○

○

Name _____

Directions: Fill in the answer bubble under the ending sound for each picture.

Tip: Remember to fill in the answer bubble completely.

d	t	b	p	x	s
○	○	○	○	○	○

n	m	g	f	s	b
○	○	○	○	○	○

r	t	d	r	g	v
○	○	○	○	○	○

Name _____

Directions: Fill in the answer bubble under the ending sound for each picture.

Tip: Remember to fill in the answer bubble completely.

Summer Link Super Edition Grade 1

Name _____

Directions: Say each picture name. Fill in the answer bubble under the vowel sound you hear.

Tip: Remember to fill in the answer bubble completely.

Summer Link Super Edition Grade 1

288

Directions: Say each picture name. Fill in the answer bubble under the vowel sound you hear.

 **Tip:** Remember to fill in the answer bubble completely.

o u e
○ ○ ○

o u e
○ ○ ○

o u e
○ ○ ○

o u e
○ ○ ○

o u e
○ ○ ○

o u e
○ ○ ○

o u e
○ ○ ○

o u e
○ ○ ○

o u e
○ ○ ○

Name _____

Directions: Look at each pair of words and pictures. Fill in the answer bubble under the pairs that rhyme.

 Tip: Remember to fill in the answer bubble completely.

   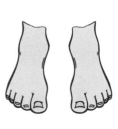

nose	hose	beet	feet
○	○	○	○

  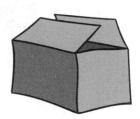 

star	jar	box	fox
○	○	○	○

dish	fish	cake	cap
○	○	○	○

Name _____

Directions: Find the small picture that shows what will happen after the pictures in the large boxes. Fill in its answer bubble.

Tip: Remember to fill in the answer bubble completely.

○

○

Name _____

Directions: Find the small picture that shows what will happen after the pictures in the large boxes. Fill in its answer bubble.

Tip: Remember to fill in the answer bubble completely.

○   ○

Name _____

Directions: Find the small picture that shows what happened right before the pictures in the large boxes. Fill in its answer bubble.

 **Tip:** Remember to fill in the answer bubble completely.

○

○

293   Summer Link Super Edition Grade 1

Directions: Find the picture that shows what happened first. Fill in its answer bubble.

Tip: Remember to fill in the answer bubble completely.

○   ○

○   ○

Directions: Fill in the answer bubble under the first thing in each row.

Tip: Remember to fill in the answer bubble completely.

○   ○   ○   ○

○   ○   ○

Name _____

Directions: Fill in the answer bubble under the second thing in each row.

 **Tip:** Remember to fill in the answer bubble completely.

○   ○   ○

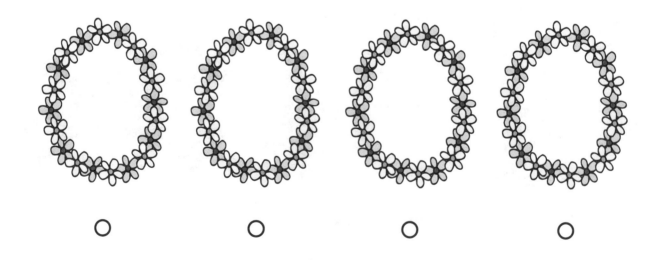

○   ○   ○   ○

Name _____

Directions: Fill in the answer bubble under the third thing in each row.

 Tip: Remember to fill in the answer bubble completely.

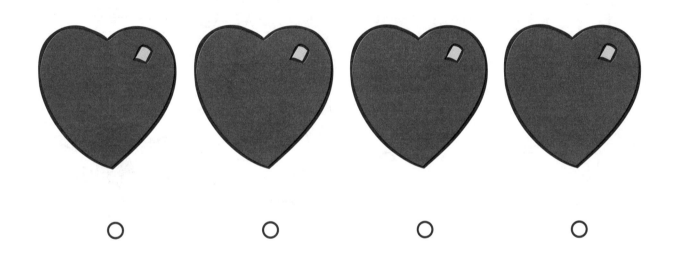

    ○   ○   ○   ○

  ○   ○   ○

Summer Link Super Edition Grade 1

Directions: Fill in the answer bubble under the last thing in each row.

Tip: Remember to fill in the answer bubble completely.

○   ○   ○   ○   ○

○   ○   ○   ○

Name _____

Directions: Fill in the answer bubble under the group in each box that has more.

Tip: Remember to fill in the answer bubble completely.

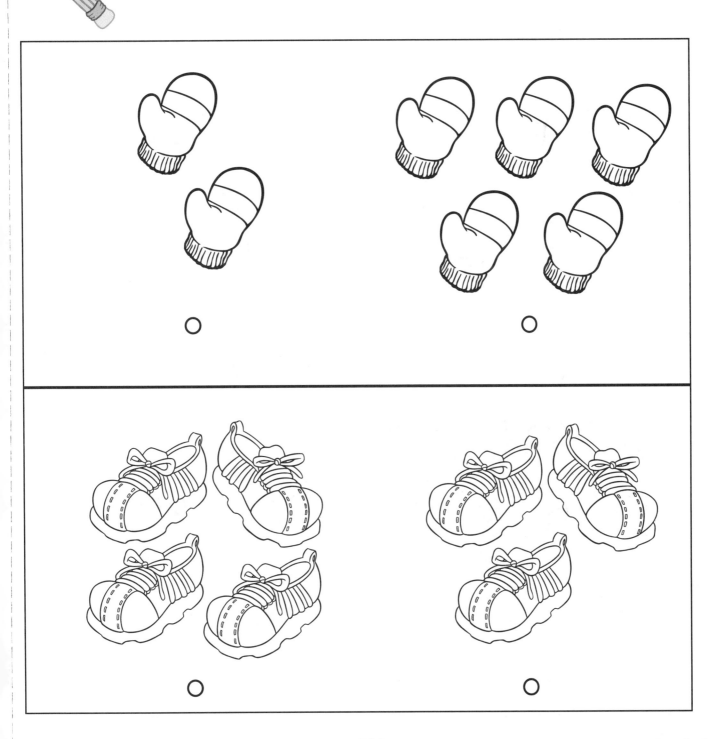

Summer Link Super Edition Grade 1

Directions: Fill in the answer bubble under the group in each box that has fewer.

Tip: Remember to fill in the answer bubble completely.

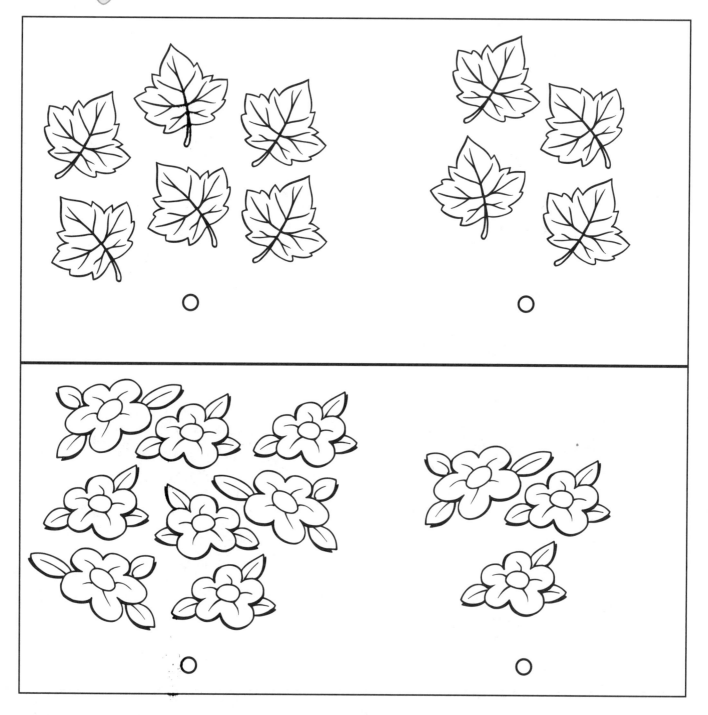

Directions: Fill in the answer bubble under the tank with zero fish in each row.

Tip: Remember to fill in the answer bubble completely.

○   ○

○   ○

Name _____

Directions: Look at the picture. Read the questions and fill in the correct answer bubbles.

Tip: Remember to fill in the answer bubble completely.

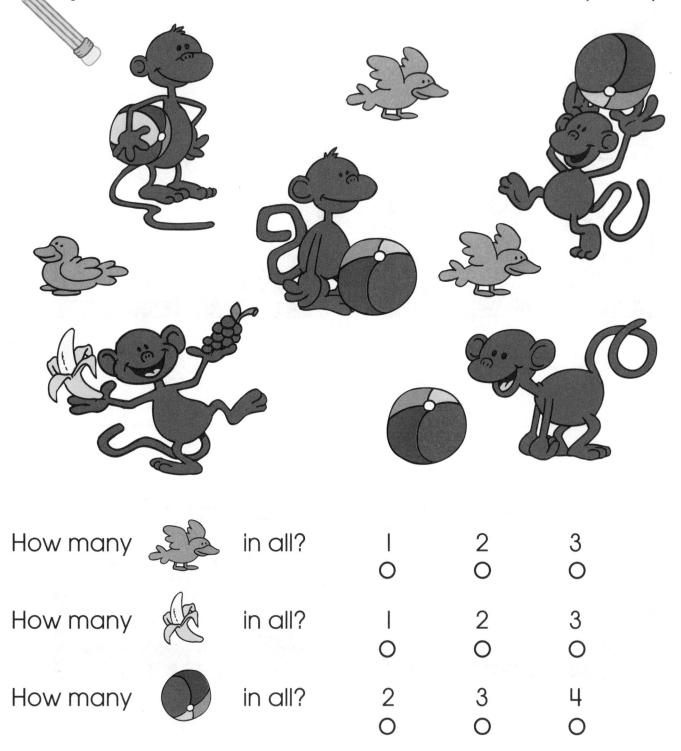

How many	🐦	in all?	1 ○	2 ○	3 ○
How many	🍌	in all?	1 ○	2 ○	3 ○
How many	⚽	in all?	2 ○	3 ○	4 ○

Name _____

Directions: Count the number in each box. Fill in the correct answer bubble for each one.

Tip: Remember to fill in the answer bubble completely.

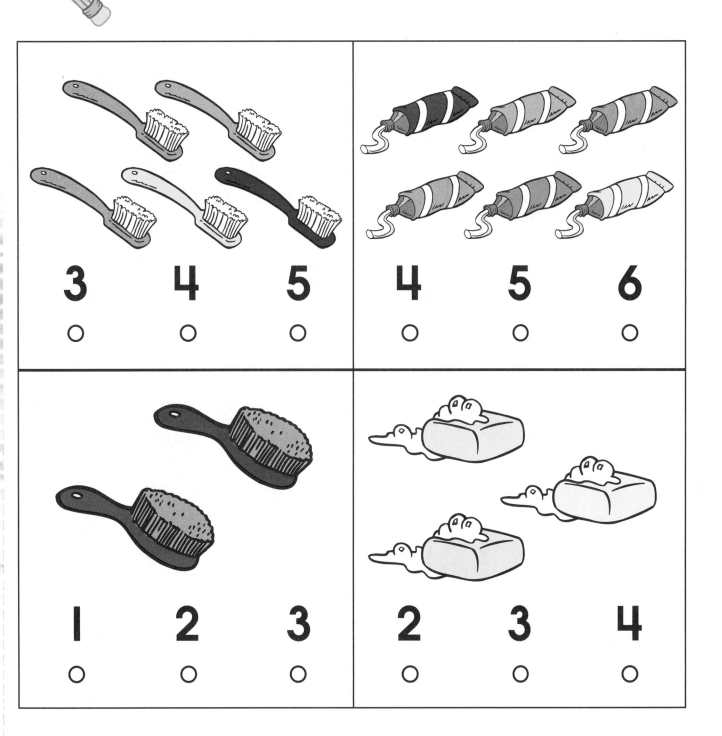

Summer Link Super Edition Grade 1

Directions: Count the number in each box. Fill in the correct answer bubble for each one.

Tip: Remember to fill in the answer bubble completely.

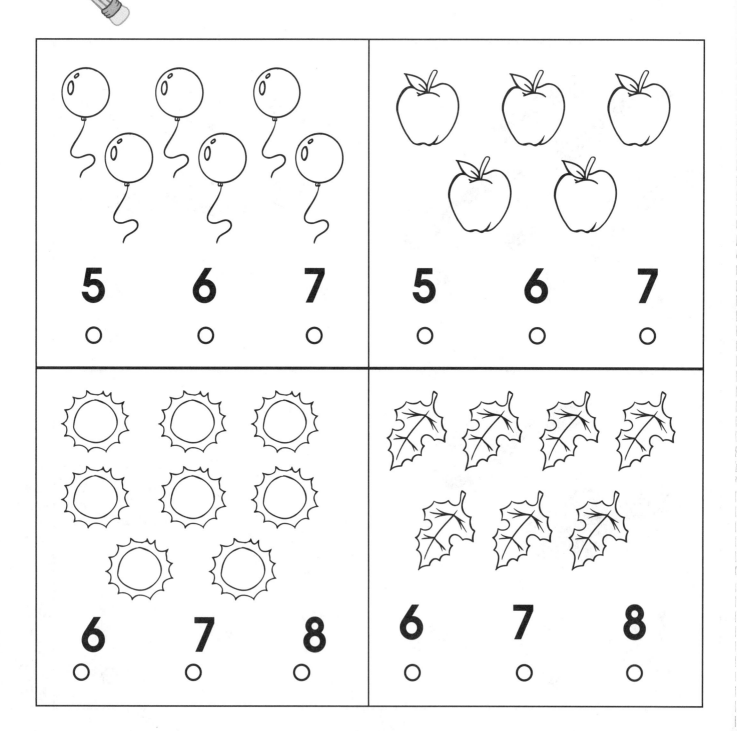

| 5 | 6 | 7 |
| ○ | ○ | ○ |

| 5 | 6 | 7 |
| ○ | ○ | ○ |

| 6 | 7 | 8 |
| ○ | ○ | ○ |

| 6 | 7 | 8 |
| ○ | ○ | ○ |

Name _____

Directions: Count the number in each box. Fill in the correct answer bubble for each one.

Tip: Remember to fill in the answer bubble completely.

8	9	10
○	○	○

8	9	10
○	○	○

8	9	10
○	○	○

8	9	10
○	○	○

Name _____

Directions: Count the number in each box. Fill in the correct answer bubble for each one.

Tip: Remember to fill in the answer bubble completely.

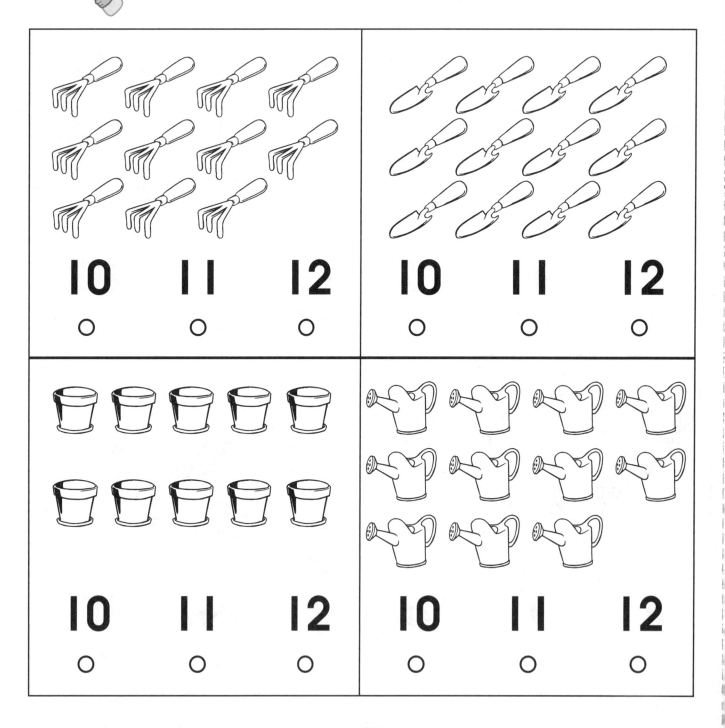

Name _____

Directions: Fill in the answer bubble under the correct amount of money in each row.

 **Tip:** Remember to fill in the answer bubble completely.

	2¢ ○	**3¢** ○	**4¢** ○

	5¢ ○	**6¢** ○	**7¢** ○

	8¢ ○	**9¢** ○	**10¢** ○

	9¢ ○	**10¢** ○	**11¢** ○

Summer Link Super Edition Grade 1

PAGE 257

Directions: Fill in the answer bubble under the circle in each row.

Tip: Remember to fill in the answer bubble completely.

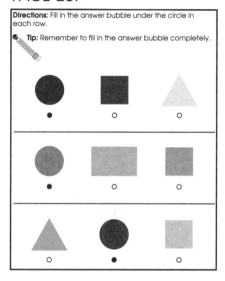

PAGE 258

Directions: Fill in the answer bubble under the square in each row.

Tip: Remember to fill in the answer bubble completely.

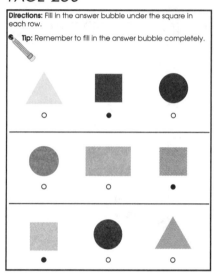

PAGE 259

Directions: Fill in the answer bubble under the triangle in each row.

Tip: Remember to fill in the answer bubble completely.

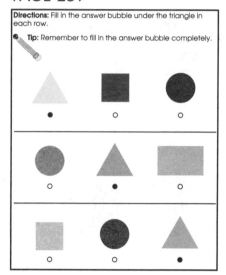

PAGE 260

Directions: Fill in the answer bubble under the rectangle in each row.

Tip: Remember to fill in the answer bubble completely.

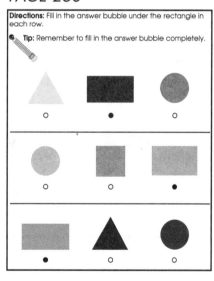

PAGE 261

Tip: Remember to fill in the answer bubble completely.

Directions: Fill in the answer bubble under the circle.

Fill in the answer bubble under the square.

Fill in the answer bubble under the triangle.

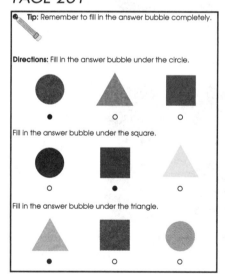

PAGE 262

Directions: Fill in the answer bubble under the oval in each row.

Tip: Remember to fill in the answer bubble completely.

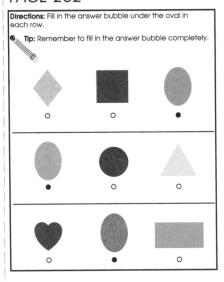

PAGE 263

Directions: Fill in the answer bubble under the diamond in each row.

Tip: Remember to fill in the answer bubble completely.

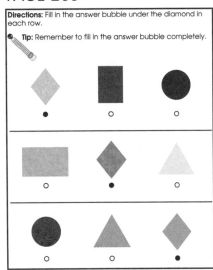

PAGE 264

Directions: Fill in the answer bubble under the star in each row.

Tip: Remember to fill in the answer bubble completely.

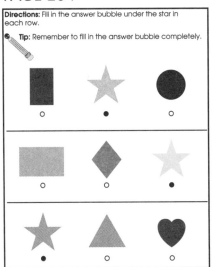

PAGE 265

Directions: Fill in the answer bubble under the heart in each row.

Tip: Remember to fill in the answer bubble completely.

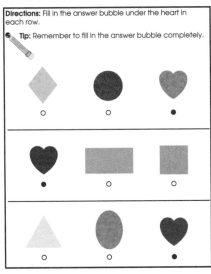

PAGE 266

Directions: Fill in the answer bubble under the shape in each row that is different.

Tip: Remember to fill in the answer bubble completely.

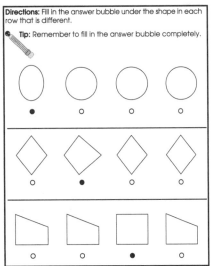

PAGE 267

Directions: Find the shape in each row that looks the same as the first shape. Fill in its answer bubble.

Tip: Remember to fill in the answer bubble completely.

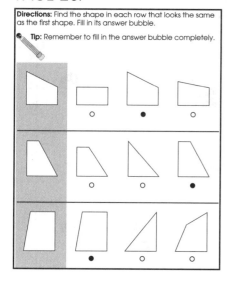

PAGE 268

Directions: Find the picture in each row that does not belong. Fill in its answer bubble.

Tip: Remember to fill in the answer bubble completely.

PAGE 269

Directions: Find the picture in each row that does not belong. Fill in its answer bubble.

Tip: Remember to fill in the answer bubble completely.

PAGE 270

Tip: Remember to fill in the answer bubble completely.

Directions: Fill in the answer bubble under the picture that is small.

Fill in the answer bubble under the picture that is big.

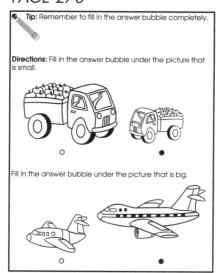

PAGE 271

Tip: Remember to fill in the answer bubble completely.

Directions: Find the picture that is above the cloud. Fill in its answer bubble.

Find the picture that is below the cloud. Fill in its answer bubble.

PAGE 272

Directions: Find the shape that is between the other shapes. Fill in its answer bubble.

✏️ **Tip:** Remember to fill in the answer bubble completely.

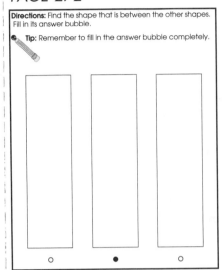

○　　●　　○

PAGE 273

✏️ **Tip:** Remember to fill in the answer bubble completely.

Directions: Fill in the answer bubble under the picture on the left.

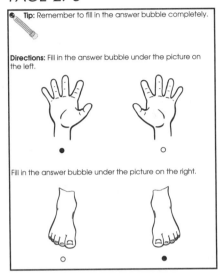

●　　　　○

Fill in the answer bubble under the picture on the right.

○　　　　●

PAGE 274

Directions: Fill in the answer bubble under the letter that matches the first letter in each row.

✏️ **Tip:** Remember to fill in the answer bubble completely.

A	N ○	V ○	A ●
a	b ○	c ○	a ●
B	B ●	C ○	A ○
b	d ○	a ○	b ●
C	O ○	D ○	C ●
c	a ○	c ●	o ○

PAGE 275

Directions: Fill in the answer bubble under the letter that matches the first letter in each row.

✏️ **Tip:** Remember to fill in the answer bubble completely.

D	B ○	G ○	D ●
d	b ○	d ●	a ○
E	H ○	F ○	E ●
e	e ●	a ○	b ○
F	E ○	F ●	A ○
f	t ○	f ●	l ○

PAGE 276

Directions: Fill in the answer bubble under the letter that matches the first letter in each row.

✏️ **Tip:** Remember to fill in the answer bubble completely.

G	C ○	G ●	O ○
g	g ●	p ○	q ○
H	E ○	F ○	H ●
h	n ○	b ○	h ●
I	H ○	I ●	L ○
i	t ○	i ●	l ○

PAGE 277

Directions: Fill in the answer bubble under the letter that matches the first letter in each row.

✏️ **Tip:** Remember to fill in the answer bubble completely.

J	J ●	U ○	L ○
j	g ○	j ●	i ○
K	N ○	H ○	K ●
k	h ○	k ●	b ○
L	J ○	I ○	L ●
I	t ○	i ○	I ●

PAGE 278

Directions: Fill in the answer bubble under the letter that matches the first letter in each row.

✏️ **Tip:** Remember to fill in the answer bubble completely.

M	H ○	M ●	L ○
m	M ○	m ●	n ○
N	M ○	N ●	m ○
n	n ●	m ○	a ○
O	O ●	D ○	B ○
o	a ○	O ○	o ●

PAGE 279

Directions: Fill in the answer bubble under the letter that matches the first letter in each row.

✏️ **Tip:** Remember to fill in the answer bubble completely.

P	D ○	P ●	b ○
p	p ●	d ○	b ○
Q	O ○	G ○	Q ●
q	p ○	q ●	d ○
R	B ○	P ○	R ●
r	n ○	m ○	r ●

PAGE 280

Directions: Fill in the answer bubble under the letter that matches the first letter in each row.

✏️ **Tip:** Remember to fill in the answer bubble completely.

S	P ○	S ●	B ○
s	a ○	s ●	e ○
T	I ○	L ○	T ●
t	f ○	t ●	i ○
U	D ○	U ●	O ○
u	u ●	n ○	m ○

PAGE 281

Directions: Fill in the answer bubble under the letter that matches the first letter in each row.

✏️ **Tip:** Remember to fill in the answer bubble completely.

V	W ○	V ●	A ○
v	w ○	v ●	y ○
W	V ○	M ○	W ●
w	w ●	v ○	x ○
X	Y ○	X ●	K ○
x	y ○	x ●	z ○

PAGE 282

Directions: Fill in the answer bubble under the letter that matches the first letter in each row.

Tip: Remember to fill in the answer bubble completely.

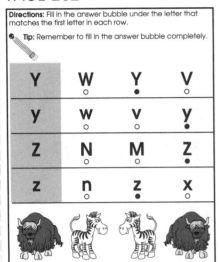

PAGE 283

Directions: Fill in the answer bubble under each fish that has an uppercase and lowercase letter that match.

Tip: Remember to fill in the answer bubble completely.

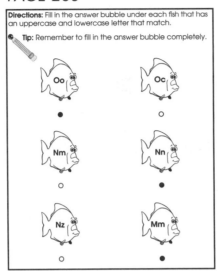

PAGE 284

Directions: Find the picture in each row that begins with the letter shown. Fill in its answer bubble.

Tip: Remember to fill in the answer bubble completely.

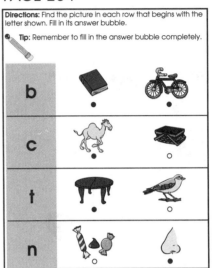

PAGE 285

Directions: Find the picture in each row that has the same beginning sound as the colored picture. Fill in its answer bubble.

Tip: Remember to fill in the answer bubble completely.

PAGE 286

Directions: Fill in the answer bubble under the ending sound for each picture.

Tip: Remember to fill in the answer bubble completely.

PAGE 287

Directions: Fill in the answer bubble under the ending sound for each picture.

Tip: Remember to fill in the answer bubble completely.

t ○ p ●	n ● b ○	b ○ t ●
n ○ p ●	p ○ b ●	p ○ t ●
b ● p ○	n ○ p ●	t ● n ○

PAGE 288

Directions: Say each picture name. Fill in the answer bubble under the vowel sound you hear.

Tip: Remember to fill in the answer bubble completely.

a ● i ○	a ● i ○	a ○ i ●
a ● i ○	a ○ i ●	a ● i ○
a ○ i ●	a ○ i ●	a ○ i ●

PAGE 289

Directions: Say each picture name. Fill in the answer bubble under the vowel sound you hear.

Tip: Remember to fill in the answer bubble completely.

o ● u ○ e ○	o ● u ○ e ○	o ○ u ○ e ●
o ● u ○ e ○	o ○ u ○ e ●	o ○ u ● e ○
o ○ u ● e ○	o ○ u ● e ○	o ○ u ● e ○

PAGE 290

Directions: Look at each pair of words and pictures. Fill in the answer bubble under the pairs that rhyme.

Tip: Remember to fill in the answer bubble completely.

nose ● hose ●	beet ● feet ●	
star ● jar ●	box ● fox ●	
dish ● fish ●	cake ○ cap ○	

PAGE 291

Directions: Find the small picture that shows what will happen after the pictures in the large boxes. Fill in its answer bubble.

Tip: Remember to fill in the answer bubble completely.

○   ●

PAGE 292

Directions: Find the small picture that shows what will happen after the pictures in the large boxes. Fill in its answer bubble.

Tip: Remember to fill in the answer bubble completely.

PAGE 293

Directions: Find the small picture that shows what happened right before the pictures in the large boxes. Fill in its answer bubble.

Tip: Remember to fill in the answer bubble completely.

PAGE 294

Directions: Find the picture that shows what happened first. Fill in its answer bubble.

Tip: Remember to fill in the answer bubble completely.

PAGE 295

Directions: Fill in the answer bubble under the first thing in each row.

Tip: Remember to fill in the answer bubble completely.

PAGE 296

Directions: Fill in the answer bubble under the second thing in each row.

Tip: Remember to fill in the answer bubble completely.

PAGE 297

Directions: Fill in the answer bubble under the third thing in each row.

Tip: Remember to fill in the answer bubble completely.

PAGE 298

Directions: Fill in the answer bubble under the last thing in each row.

Tip: Remember to fill in the answer bubble completely.

PAGE 299

Directions: Fill in the answer bubble under the group in each box that has more.

Tip: Remember to fill in the answer bubble completely.

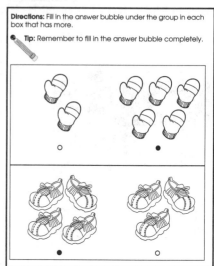

PAGE 300

Directions: Fill in the answer bubble under the group in each box that has fewer.

Tip: Remember to fill in the answer bubble completely.

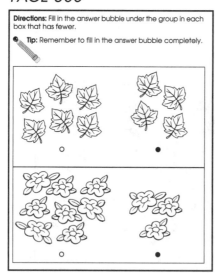

PAGE 301

Directions: Fill in the answer bubble under the tank with zero fish in each row.

Tip: Remember to fill in the answer bubble completely.

PAGE 302

Directions: Look at the picture. Read the questions and fill in the correct answer bubbles.

✏️ **Tip:** Remember to fill in the answer bubble completely.

How many 🕊 in all?	1 ○	2 ○	3 ●
How many 🍌 in all?	1 ●	2 ○	3 ○
How many ⚽ in all?	2 ○	3 ○	4 ●

PAGE 303

Directions: Count the number in each box. Fill in the correct answer bubble for each one.

✏️ **Tip:** Remember to fill in the answer bubble completely.

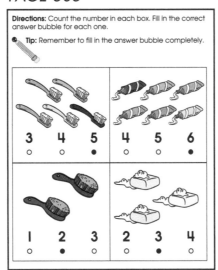

PAGE 304

Directions: Count the number in each box. Fill in the correct answer bubble for each one.

✏️ **Tip:** Remember to fill in the answer bubble completely.

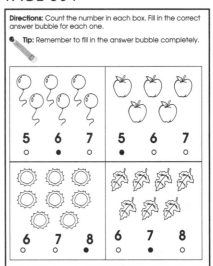

PAGE 305

Directions: Count the number in each box. Fill in the correct answer bubble for each one.

✏️ **Tip:** Remember to fill in the answer bubble completely.

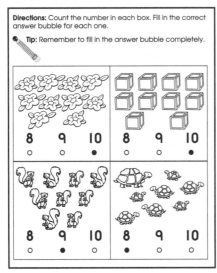

PAGE 306

Directions: Count the number in each box. Fill in the correct answer bubble for each one.

✏️ **Tip:** Remember to fill in the answer bubble completely.

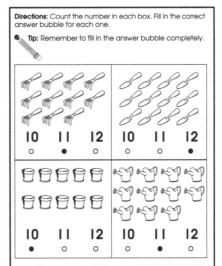

PAGE 307

Directions: Fill in the answer bubble under the correct amount of money in each row.

Tip: Remember to fill in the answer bubble completely.

	2¢ ○	3¢ ●	4¢ ○
	5¢ ○	6¢ ○	7¢ ●
	8¢ ○	9¢ ●	10¢ ○
	9¢ ○	10¢ ○	11¢ ●

Test Practice Worksheet

Test Practice Worksheet